M000087924

"No more excuses, Canadians. With *The Value of Simple*, John explains not only the theory behind the best way for you to invest, but also provides easy-to-understand step-by-step guides to show precisely how simple it is to implement these investing strategies. The book gives everyday Canadians easy-to-implement ways to invest that will take you from procrastinating neophyte investor to confident portfolio manager in an afternoon or two of straightforward reading. If my high school students can immediately understand these Canadian-specific ways to invest, so can you!"

—Kyle Prevost, Co-author of *More Money for Beer and Textbooks,* and Freelance Personal Finance Writer

"Outstanding. There is nothing wrong with this book and lots and lots of things right with it."

—Sandi Martin, Financial Planner
Spring Plans (www.springplans.ca),
Co-host of *Because Money* (becausemoney.ca)

"The best part is that I feel much more confident and knowledgeable in my investments than I ever did with the bank-recommended mutual funds that I held onto before. This book is a must-read for anyone wanting to take control of their financial future!"

—Jill Bressmer, Small Business Owner

"I'm of the opinion most professions tend to make the simple overly complex. The financial industry is no exception to this. *The Value of Simple* outlines the reasons for saving (most of them you already know) but then provides some solid "how-to" steps to make it happen – a feat few personal finance and investing books take on."

—Mark Seed, myownadvisor.ca

"The author describes the investing process in a way that's rarely explained – taking a step-by-step approach to show investors exactly what they need to do in order to start building and maintaining a portfolio of low-cost index funds. This book is for investors who are looking to take the plunge into DIY investing and want a guide to help walk them through the process from start to finish."

—Robb Engen, Finance Columnist and Financial Planner
Boomer & Echo (boomerandecho.com)

"I highly recommend this book to anyone who feels confused about how to invest."

—Michael J. Wiener, michaeljamesonmoney.com

"The 'explain it like I'm 5' (ELI5) guide to investing. No other book has a step-by-step guide when it comes to making your first investment so you really have no excuse for not getting started."

—Barry Choi, moneywehave.com

"Brilliantly simple and simply brilliant!"

—Shubh, reader in Toronto

"*The Value of Simple* is the only investing book I've read that actually teaches you how to invest. Many books tell you why, John shows you *how*. I picked it up with the intention of quickly skimming through 'the important bits' and ended up binge-reading the whole thing cover-to-cover (while on vacation!!). He breaks it down step-by-step and somehow manages to address every single, 'Ya, but what about...?!' question that other finance books I'd read would gloss over. Investing my own money finally felt like something I could do... and I now am!"

—Kate Smalley, katesmalley.com

"This is simply the best book to read if you want to start investing and feel overwhelmed."

—Chris Enns, Financial Planner, ragstoreasonable.com
Co-host of *Because Money* (becausemoney.ca)

"A good book is the kind that saves you from having to read ten others. This is that kind of book."

—Scott, reader in Ottawa

"Your book has become my bible for investing. Honestly – nothing comes close for beginners like me!"

—Heath, reader in BC

The Value of Simple

A Practical Guide to Taking the Complexity Out of Investing

Second Edition

John Robertson, PhD

© 2018

THE VALUE OF SIMPLE

A Practical Guide to Taking
the Complexity Out of Investing

Second Edition

John Robertson, PhD

Copyright © 2014, 2018 by John Robertson. All rights reserved.

Blessed by the Potato Publishing
Toronto, Ontario, Canada
http://www.holypotato.net

ISBN 978-0-9878189-3-5

This is the second edition of *The Value of Simple: A Practical Guide to Taking the Complexity Out of Investing* – first edition ISBN 978-0-9878189-1-1 and 978-0-9878189-2-8. Cover design by Ben Pakuts.

Errata: For information and corrections released after the publication of this book, please see https://valueofsimple.ca/errata For convenience, links referenced in the text have also been collected on the site.

Disclaimer: *This book discusses investment strategies and products in a general sense as an educational resource. Investing involves various risks: you may lose money. Past results do not guarantee future performance. Readers will hold the author free from any responsibility, and adapt the general suggestions and examples to their specific situation as required.*

This book is not intended as individualized investment advice, nor as a solicitation or recommendation to buy or sell any securities or investment product. You may need to seek the services of a professional before making any investment decisions.

This work incorporates screenshots from several providers; the content of these screenshots may contain trademarks and logos of Tangerine, TD Canada Trust, or Questrade. Trademarks and logos belong to their respective owners.

Prologue

Hello there, I'm glad you decided to give this book a read. I hope you'll find it welcoming, understandable, and above all, *useful*. If you're excited and eager to start learning about do-it-yourself investing, then I might suggest you skip the rest of this and go straight to the table of contents. If you need to summon up your courage a bit more, keep reading.

Investing can be a scary thing. There are entire TV stations dedicated to the topic, yet for many it's completely unfamiliar. It can be technical with its own language, and requires a long-term perspective unlike the rest of everyday life. It also looks suspiciously like math in places. But it doesn't have to be scary and technical; you can be quite successful at investing while letting it *stay* largely unfamiliar. You can set up a simple, easy-to-follow plan in just a few hours, and then get on with the rest of your life – and walking you through that is exactly what this book is about. Taking the first step and making the decision to invest on your own is likely going to be the hardest part. That's why I started this book with this friendly little page: the casual tone should be a clear sign that you won't be overwhelmed by technical details here.

There's no one right answer when it comes to managing your money, just as there's no one right answer for the other aspects of how you live your life. However, research shows that when faced with too many options, some people may become paralyzed by the choice and rather than pick *something* that's at least *good enough* and move on, they will instead dither and end up with nothing. So in many places I'm going to limit the number of options I present by using my judgement to narrow things down to the few that I think are most likely to help you, recognizing the value of simple; anything that adds complexity has to be *worth* that extra effort.

Investing really can be easy, and I mean *actually* easy, not like dieting where they *say* it's easy – just eat less – but hard to actually pull off in practice.

There is inevitably *some* math involved with money, but you don't need anything more complex than what you learned in grade school, and even then we'll get spreadsheet programs to do the hard work for us.

You can do this. And just in case, I'm going to borrow from Douglas Adams here and put a big, friendly message on the next page. Turn back to read it again whenever you need to.

Don't Panic

John Robertson

Table of Contents

John Robertson

On Exponential Growth, Bunnies, and the Future

Introduction

Choosing to keep things as simple as possible will help maximize your chances of success. Complexity leads to indecision, an increased chance of making mistakes, and a loss of confidence. There is value in *simple*. This is as true for investing as it is for any other aspect of your life.

Learning any complex physical skill is difficult at first, with lots of conscious thought required to make anything happen, and you will make lots of errors. But it gets easier and more accurate with practice, because as you work at it processes in your cerebellum and spinal cord take over many of the individual muscle controls – you build "muscle memory." These processes and automation are an important evolutionary feature for managing complexity – the skills and movements of your body are just as complex, but the processing burden on your brain is reduced by breaking the movement down into simple, automatic components.

In investing, we do not have the luxury of taking multiple attempts at it and suffering repeated failures to build internal skill. Fortunately, we can use processes to help automate some parts of investing, and incorporate the lessons learned by the past. Much of the complexity can be ignored in favour of focusing on just the few factors that truly matter and can be controlled.

Good *processes* are critical. Investing is something you will be doing for the rest of your life, but it shouldn't *become* your life. Once set up, your processes will help you stay on track without a lot of ongoing effort.

Your car has thousands of moving parts, yet you get where you want to go by focusing on just three simple controls. Many of the parts and fluids wear out and need to be maintained or replaced before they fail. Each has its own individual expected lifetime, but the engineers have simplified maintenance procedures into just a handful of options on a menu at regular mileage intervals that are good enough for most cars in the fleet. Complexity can be effectively managed by non-experts with the right tools and processes – and to extend the metaphor, with the occasional expert check-up.

There are lots of books on finance and investing in the world, and I won't pretend that they don't exist. However, they do miss one important aspect: *how* are you supposed to take the information they give and actually start investing? It is the question I've been asked time and again after people read other leading investing books yet still aren't clear on how to take the general, somewhat academic information they contain and move on to implementing a financial plan. The reason I sat down to write this book was to fill in those gaps in implementation and walk you through the process of investing.

It was important to keep the book short: ideally you should be able to plow through it, devise, and then implement your financial plan while you're still on a kick to do it and while all the information is fresh in your head. Short is also important because a major barrier that prevents people from getting started in investing is a lack of time. The passive (or "index") investing approach I will lay out requires minimal effort to maintain: likely just a few hours per year.

However, those very benefits mean that you're likely to forget many of the finer details between your yearly check-ups. The processes and lessons in this book are designed so that you won't need refreshers at all because it will just simply *work*. Though just in case, you should place the book in a hallowed and handy spot on your bookshelf for the quick refreshers to come.

When you develop your process you have to keep in mind that your future self may be years or decades removed from having done all the reading and research you're doing right now. This book will help you set things up to be easy-to-manage, with explicit instructions to your future self. On top of that, I encourage you to take notes on what you decide to do as well as *why* you decided it; how you came to a decision may help you decide if you need to revise it later.

This book was built and refined over the course of years, working side-by-side with novice investors to identify common barriers, and what was needed to help give them the confidence to invest on their own. Investing and finance have their own technical jargon, and that language barrier is one that processes alone won't shatter. I am trained as a scientist – my PhD is in Medical Biophysics – and in my career I have focused on scientific communications: how to effectively communicate highly technical information to people without expertise in it. Explaining complex things so they seem simple is my particular speciality.

In the fine print at the beginning (along with the ISBN and copyright notice), I included a web address for the errata page[1]. Please do check it as the years go on: a lot

---

[1] Here it is again: http://www.valueofsimple.ca

can change in a short amount of time in the investing world. In the spring of 2014, as I was busy composing this book, the commission costs for small accounts were slashed at the brokerage arms of several of Canada's big banks and fund providers started a small price war on fund costs. More changes are sure to come, and I'll make note of them on that page as they do. All of the hyperlinks referenced in the book are also collected there for convenience.

I will note that this book is focused on investing and creating a financial plan for the long term. In the grand spectrum of personal finance this material is typically somewhere around step three; after getting out of debt and budgeting. How to create a household budget and spend less than you earn so that you have some savings to invest in the first place is important; knowing what you spend to live – even approximately – is going to be essential for long-term planning.

This book is broken down into three major parts:

- First, I will introduce the basic building blocks that you will use in building your financial plan and investment portfolio, things like what you can invest in, where you can put those investments, some basics on how taxes and tax shelters work, and what to think about when you create your long-term plan.

- Second will come the step-by-step practical section, which will walk you through how to open accounts and purchase investments for three specific investing options. It will also provide the tools and methods to track and maintain your portfolio.

- Third, I will bring us around to revisit some of the more advanced issues and special situations, including some common (and unending) debates in personal finance.

The Framework of the Story – Part 1: Investing

Investing basically means using your money to buy something that will *most likely* provide you with more money in the future: through growth, interest payments, income, or dividends. You have your money earning more money, either by lending it out for a period of time and collecting interest (as with a savings account, GIC, or bond), buying part of a profitable business (i.e. stock/equity), or making a business for yourself (like buying an apartment to rent out or investing in the tools you need to make something you can sell).

The two key factors to investing are your rate of return and time. Time is an easy one to understand: the sooner you start saving and investing, the better off you'll be. Give that compound interest enough time to act, and eventually the accumulated returns will dwarf the initial savings. If you start saving when you're 30, over half your nest egg at 65 will be from investment returns even with just a 3% return. With an 8% return, your nest egg will be five times what it would be if you had kept your money under the mattress.

This example also highlights the importance of your rate of return. Though it is possible to save up for a secure retirement using just low-rate guaranteed investments like savings accounts and GICs, almost all the money you have at the end will be the product of your work from saving, rather than from getting your money to work for you. Being able to count on a higher return means you won't have to be quite so strict in your budgeting during your working years[2].

You can get a much better long-term return by investing in stocks, but you have to be willing to take on the risks. The risks include not knowing what your return will be in advance; having those returns be inconsistent; and facing the risk of losing money, particularly in the short term. But there is risk in everything: savings accounts may not keep up with inflation for instance. With patience and a long life ahead of you, taking those risks will be well rewarded. We'll get into the details of risk later.

Getting started early definitely has an advantage. If you started at 30, saving $10,000 per year and earning 6%, you'd have $1.2 million built up by age 65, which should fund a very nice, secure retirement. Starting later, even increasing the amount saved each year to get the same total of contributed savings, you'd find that starting at 50 would leave you with half as much by 65 ($578,000), and you'd have to save more than twice as much ($22,500/year) to get even that.

However, these things are only somewhat under your control: you can start investing now, but you may not be able to keep working into old age. Aside from choosing to invest in assets that will most likely have higher returns, your rate of return is also out of your control.

You shouldn't expose yourself to any risk you don't understand and aren't prepared to accept. But including stocks in your portfolio (or mutual funds that hold a collection of stocks) is a good option for most people; a

---

[2] This is a very dangerous thing for me to say, but it's also an important and true point to make. Please don't fall into the trap of saving less by assuming too high a rate of return only to end up disappointed.

lack of knowledge or fear of the unknown shouldn't be a barrier that keeps you out. Get out there and do your homework (reading the rest of this book is a good place to start)!

Start saving, start investing. Get your money working for you *now*.

The Framework of the Story – Part 2: Fees

Now that you know that investing is going to be important for your future self, why *do it yourself?* There are people out there throwing themselves at you, eager to manage your money for you. Representatives at your local bank branch, planners with wealth management companies, and independent brokers are standing by to take your call now, with ads plastered over bus benches and on TV. Going with one of them would certainly save time, and avoid all the hassle of learning terminology you'll never use again and engaging with what looked *suspiciously* like math on the previous page.

But stop and ask yourself why there are so many people eager to free you of this burden. There's quite a bit of money to be made in it, and they make that money at your expense. The mutual funds you buy all have fees associated with them. These fees are hidden[3] – you don't get a bill for them every month, but they're there to be sure, disclosed in the funds' prospectus as a "management fee" or "management expense ratio" (**MER**). The average mutual fund fee in Canada is nearly 2.5% per year, part of which usually goes to the institution that runs the fund itself, and part of which is paid as a commission to whoever sold the fund to you.

Indeed, many would-be advisors are not strictly speaking working purely in your best interest: they get paid for putting you into certain products, and that

---

[3] Changes to fee disclosures were made in recent years to make part of these fees less hidden, and expressed in dollars, but there is still room for improvement in fee transparency in Canada.

commission may influence their recommendations, particularly when it comes time to recommending that you switch around your investments. The standard-of-care in Canada is a "suitability requirement," which means that funds advisors recommend have to fit within what they know of a client's plans and risk tolerance. However, a bond fund that charges a 0.5% MER and one with the same holdings that charges 2.5% (kicking back 1% to the advisor as a commission) are equally suitable under that requirement in a legal sense, though perhaps you will agree that in a real sense that's not at all the case.

This commission is supposed to pay for their advice and assistance in helping you create a financial plan. However, many people you may see across the desk from you at a bank branch or investment firm are actually in a sales role and don't end up providing any help in overall guidance or long-term planning, or provide poor, self-serving advice. The conflict-of-interest where they only get paid if you invest in the mutual funds they have to sell means that they may recommend investing even if paying down your debt might be in your best interest instead.

Some fees are unavoidable in investing – you will never find a fund with a 0% MER – but it *is* possible to get a low-cost fund at around 0.5%, versus a more typical Canadian fund at nearly 2.5%. So let's say that the excess cost of a typical mutual fund is 2%. The math on that is pretty easy to do: for every $100 you have invested, you pay $2 a year in fees. Even for someone just a few years into saving for retirement with a few tens of thousands to invest that can represent hundreds of dollars a year lost to fees – and at that stage of your life, your time is probably not so valuable that you'd pay someone that much to avoid doing the work yourself; a few hundred extra may make a significant dent in your savings plan. Later on those fees can amount to thousands of dollars each year when you have hundreds of thousands to invest.

Paying for people's time and expertise is not inherently wrong, but you have to be sure that you get value for the money that you pay, and sadly that is not the case in much of the financial industry in Canada. There is a large focus on investing and choosing funds when you sit in front of an "advisor" though this is where they add the least amount of value. Many people would be better served by discussing spending, saving, emergency plans, and charting a long-term course. The fact that the fees are hidden helps mask the fact that you may not be getting value: by not explicitly billing for advice or including it as a line item in your statement your brain can be fooled into thinking that your advisor is just a friend helping you out. In that context, less-than-optimal service is easily forgivable. But once you realize that an advisor is getting paid out of your returns – often quite handsomely – without sharing the risk, then you may demand the very best in planning service, and rightfully expect it.

Taking a low-cost do-it-yourself approach to investing and paying – on a transparent flat or hourly rate – for help in crafting a long-term plan may be the best of both worlds. See "Getting Help" on page 195 for more on how to find professional help without the conflicts-of-interest presented by commission-based compensation.

How big an influence is this MER on your overall returns? After all, 2.5% doesn't sound like much. Yet given enough time to compound – like the better part of your adult life until well into retirement – that constant drain has a big effect. Just look at the graph on the next page. Over 35 years, investing in a group of stocks[4] would

---

[4] In this case I'm using the Dow Jones Industrial Average (DJIA). This is a group of 30 large companies in the US. Rounded to nearest 10%, excluding dividends.

have given a return of over 1880%. Doing so through a low-cost mutual fund with a MER of 0.5% would have returned almost as much: 1560%. But a fund with a 2.5% MER would have only returned 720%. That seemingly harmless extra 2% per year drag ended up consuming almost half of the gains over the long term!

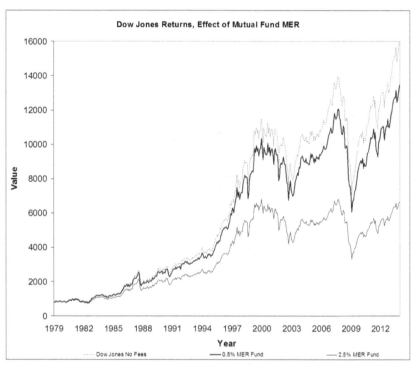

The effect of fees on returns over the long term. Inspired by a figure from Michael Wiener. Here the returns for the DJIA and a simulated mutual fund with a 0.5% and 2.5% MER are compared. The 2.5% MER ends up costing almost a third of the total returns. www.michaeljamesonmoney.com/2009/12/mer-drag-on-returns-in-pictures.html

Or to put it yet another way, if you only expect your portfolio to return around 6-8% per year then taking 2% is like taking a quarter to a third of your returns. Now it sounds *properly* serious! Plus, even in a bad year on the market when you're losing money, the manager still takes their cut. So that is one good reason to become a do-ityourselfer: to save on fees. Fees are something to keep in mind as you read the rest of the book and begin your investing career – and most importantly, **fees are one aspect of your investments you *can* control**.

Fees are important! For mutual funds the fees are called the management expense ratio (MER) and are listed somewhere in the information sheets describing the fund. Canada has some of the highest MERs in the world, and these can dramatically reduce your long-term returns.

Math Time: The Power of Compounding

Compounding or exponential growth is a truly powerful and magical thing.

Consider bunnies: widely known for their ability to breed rapidly, and also cute and non-threatening. Let's say that if you had a collection of bunnies in your backyard that they'd double their numbers every year. So you go off and collect 2 bunnies (the detail of where you get them from is not really relevant to the money metaphor we're building here). By next year, 2 bunnies have become 4. You also collect 2 more to add, giving you 6 to start the next breeding season with. The next year you have 12 new bunnies, plus another 2 that you picked up through your own skill and effort. Again the bunnies breed and double, and to your shock and amazement by the 4th spring you're knee deep in bunnies. If they stand still enough to count you'll find you have 28, and you hadn't even set off to collect your 2 new ones for the year yet. 30 total.

If you had instead locked your bunnies up in individual cages (and please don't make me explain why this means they no longer exponentially reproduce) then you'd only have the same 2 bunnies in the 2nd year, plus then the 2 new ones you added. Continuing like this where the only growth comes from the bunnies you collect with your own hard work, you find that by the end of the four years instead of 30 bunnies, you only have 8.

You see that with exponential growth the number of things you get from the growth of what you have fairly quickly *dwarfs* the linear growth of steadily adding more things.

A bunny. They're soft and cuddly, with adorable noses and long fuzzy ears. Also an excellent model organism for discussions on exponential growth.

There is a lot of elegant math to describe this type of exponential growth, even when it happens on much longer timescales, like when the doubling takes 10 years instead of 1. You probably don't need the formulas, but in case you'd like them, here is an optional discussion.

Optional Math Section

I'm going to start with the actual math, which you may remember from high school. These next two paragraphs are indented to show just how very optional they are. Feel free to revisit the picture of Kiwi the bunny above, or skip ahead and read the rest of this section which is a bit more practical, showing you how to approximate the math with just addition, multiplication, and a spreadsheet.

For some investment return *i* with principal amount *p* invested over time *t*, the formula for the amount you have in the future *FV* is:

$$FV = p(1+i)^t$$

That assumes that the interest is a percent (for plugging into the formula remember that 1% = 0.01) and the time is in units of the number of compounding periods, so if it was a yearly return then *t* would be the number of years.

For figuring out stuff yourself you can get very close using a spreadsheet program[5] and just running through the years. Here's an example using a starting value of $10 in year 1, earning a return of 8% (so each year multiply the amount you started with by 1 + 0.08).

	A	B	C
1	Year	Formula to enter into Excel	Values
2	1	10	10.00
3	2	=B2*1.08	10.80
4	3	=B3*1.08	11.66
5	4	=B4*1.08	13.60

If you're familiar with Excel, you'll immediately see what I'm doing there. You can even use the "fill down"

---

[5] Throughout the book I use spreadsheets to help with planning and tracking. I love spreadsheets and find they help save time and effort. However, not everyone does, and if they're not your thing you don't have to use them to invest – all of the math and tracking can be done by hand with pencil and paper if that works better for you.

function to have the formulas filled in automatically once the first two rows are done.

It's also useful to look at not just how an investment would grow over time from compounding returns, but also how things are affected by adding yearly savings (or withdrawals). In that case you just add the savings to the formula, for example if on top of your initial $10 you were also saving $5 per year, you could just write the formula as =B2*1.08 +5.

And that's about as hard as it gets for math in personal finance. Percentages and compound growth.

Let's get back to the magical part of compound growth: small amounts add up over time to become large amounts. Though you can now easily calculate this yourself, here's a table showing how much each $1 of investment grows over the course of multiple years, at different rates of return:

Rate Years	1%	2%	3%	4%	5%	6%	7%	8%	9%	10%
0	1	1	1	1	1	1	1	1	1	1
1	1.01	1.02	1.03	1.04	1.05	1.06	1.07	1.08	1.09	1.10
2	1.02	1.04	1.06	1.08	1.10	1.12	1.14	1.17	1.19	1.21
3	1.03	1.06	1.09	1.12	1.16	1.19	1.23	1.26	1.30	1.33
4	1.04	1.08	1.13	1.17	1.22	1.26	1.31	1.36	1.41	1.46
5	1.05	1.10	1.16	1.22	1.28	1.34	1.40	1.47	1.54	1.61
10	1.10	1.22	1.34	1.48	1.63	1.79	1.97	2.16	2.37	2.59
15	1.16	1.35	1.56	1.80	2.08	2.40	2.76	3.17	3.64	4.18
20	1.22	1.49	1.81	2.19	2.65	3.21	3.87	4.66	5.60	6.73
25	1.28	1.64	2.09	2.67	3.39	4.29	5.43	6.85	8.62	10.8
30	1.35	1.81	2.43	3.24	4.32	5.74	7.61	10.1	13.3	17.4
35	1.42	2.00	2.81	3.95	5.52	7.69	10.7	14.8	20.4	28.1
40	1.49	2.21	3.26	4.80	7.04	10.3	15.0	21.7	31.4	45.3

For the curious, the spreadsheet used to create this is available online: valueofsimple.ca/CRTSheet.html

Of course, you'll see that the higher the return the better. Note that I didn't even plot out above 10%, I'll get into why in the section on planning and expectations. And of course the longer you have for your investments to compound, the more you'll have for when you need them: so the sooner you start, the better.

This also holds true, but in reverse, for loans or debt you may have. If you carry a balance on your credit card at 20% interest, it doesn't take long at all for that to balloon to the point where it becomes very onerous to pay back. And the longer you leave it, the worse it gets. Likewise, it's worth negotiating with the bank for even a half percentage point decrease in the rate you pay to borrow for things like student loans, mortgages, or investment loans.

Where do these compounding returns come from? Ah, that's the next section!

Bunnies are adorable and reproduce quickly, growing exponentially like compound investment returns. Compound returns are powerful, and the sooner you start getting your money to reproduce, the better off you'll be in the end!

Investing: Basic Types of Investments

There are many ways to invest in something that will make money for you: buy something then sell it for more. Lend money to someone, and collect interest. Or buy a business that does some or all of the above, and pays you a share of the profits.

You're probably already familiar with the concept of lending money and collecting interest, most likely in the form of a savings account at your bank. There, you deposit your money with the bank, and the bank pays you interest. The bank is free to use the money while it's in their possession, which is how they make the money to pay you interest.

There are a number of other ways of lending money not just to the bank but to other businesses or governments, and making interest from your investment. The most common is with a **bond**. A bond is basically a loan that has been put into a standard form that can be traded before it comes due.

Let's say that you had your money in the bank, making 1% interest. Your friend Dave comes along and says that he needs to borrow some money. You know that the bank will pay you 1% and is good for the money (guaranteed), so you want to get a little more interest from Dave because you can never be quite sure if he'll disappear into the night with your money never to be seen again. So Dave draws up a little contract on the back of a napkin promising that if he borrows $100 from you now, he'll pay you back $105 in a year, so you'll make 5% on your money.

Then you go out for nachos with your friend Katie and realize you forgot your wallet. Katie graciously pays that night, but the next day is on your doorstep with a baseball bat wanting her money.

You hope she's just on her way to baseball practice.

Still unable to find your wallet you say "Wait, wait, Dave owes me money! Just get it from Dave!" And you hand her your napkin-contract with Dave, and she goes off satisfied that you've now sold your loan from Dave to her. Katie may trade off Dave's loan to someone else, and they may trade it off yet again until when it comes due you don't even know the person that Dave has to end up paying.

That napkin is basically what a bond is: a loan that can be traded around. Bonds are issued by both governments as well as companies, and though the initial loan may be for many years, you don't necessarily have to keep your money lent out for that long if you don't want to: you can just sell the bond to someone else before it's due.

Bonds are called **fixed income** because you expect to get back the amount you lent out plus some amount of interest, with very few surprises along the way. A more common form of fixed income is a savings account at your bank, or a guaranteed investment certificate (GIC), which is like a savings account that gets locked in for a period of time (usually up to five years).

The other main type of investment is **equity**, or the ownership of a business. A business can be split up into multiple shares: in a partnership for instance, two people may each own a share of the business, with each share representing 50% ownership. For larger corporations, it's possible to split the ownership up into millions or even billions of shares. Then even someone with only a few thousand dollars to invest can own a tiny sliver of the business of a huge corporation like Suncor, Tim Horton's, or Coca-Cola.

As the business makes money, increases the stuff it owns, pays back its debt, the value of the business should go up. And because a share is just a part ownership of that business, its value goes up too. On top of the increase in value, a business may pay **dividends**[6] to its owners – a cash payment that a company makes to its shareholders as a way of distributing the income earned. Over the long term, equity investments or stocks have provided more returns than fixed income. This is in part because owning a business is more risky than lending to one: there are no guarantees of profitability, and indeed a company can go out of business and end up being worth nothing[7]. In the event that a business has to shut down operations, there is an order of priority to who gets paid back – and creditors/debtholders come before owners/stockholders. So in order to take that equity ownership risk, buyers of stock demand a premium return, called plainly enough the *risk premium.*

But though individual companies may come and go, with some performing well and others just scraping by, the economy powers on. Over time the aggregate becomes more productive, with the businesses in total making more profits and becoming more valuable.

So generally speaking, those with a lot of time to wait before getting their money back should buy businesses (shares aka stocks aka equities) because that's where the greatest return lies. However, the risks must be kept in mind – and those will be a section of their own.

---

[6] Dividends historically make up an important part of the overall return for stocks. It's not all about buy-low sell-high.

[7] You've probably heard of a few companies that have ended up being worth nothing, for one reason or another. Nortel is a very popular (and recent) Canadian example.

For publicly traded companies, shares can be easily bought and sold on stock markets or exchanges, like the TSX, NYSE, or NASDAQ[8]. There are thousands of companies to choose from, including many of the "blue chip"[9] international conglomerates you've likely purchased products from in your every day life. In aggregate, all the stocks together (*or a large subset*) are referred to as the "stock market".

There are a few basic types of investments to remember:

- Savings accounts: pay interest, low returns but easy to access.

- GICs: pay interest, both amount invested and interest guaranteed, may require locking in.

- Bonds: pay interest and in some cases may go up (or down) in price, pretty safe.

- Equities: pay dividends and may go up (or down) in price, riskiest for short-term investments but also generally provide the greatest long-term returns.

---

[8] The exact acronyms aren't important, just know that the TSX = Toronto/Canadian stock exchange, NYSE = New York/main American stock exchange, and NASDAQ = another important American stock exchange.

[9] A "blue chip" company is not precisely defined, but generally refers to large, stable companies. The term comes from poker, where the blue chips are the high value poker chips.

More on the Stock Market

I mentioned that owning shares in a business was more risky than bonds, but I never defined risk. It turns out that defining risk is actually rather complicated, because of the influence of statisticians and the fact that there are many sources of risk. Trying to precisely define risk could lead us down a dark and twisty rabbit hole. Instead, let's start from a common-sense approximate definition: a chance of losing money. That can be because of the risk that the company you invest in will turn out to not be able to make money and be worthless, and you will never get your investment back, or the risk that the price will fluctuate from day to day and happen to be down on the day that you need to sell.

Ah yes, the prices *do* fluctuate. Look up any individual stock or an aggregate stock index such as the S&P 500 or TSX: the prices move up and down chaotically day-to-day, month-to-month, and year-to-year[10]. Why is that? Well, let's step back for a second and consider what a business is *worth*. This, it turns out, is not an easy question to answer either. Entire books, indeed, entire sections of libraries, have been written on methods for answering precisely that question of what a company is worth. If you can put a price on what you would pay for the entire business, then you just have to divide that by the number of shares to get a price for the shares.

For example, let's say that Company X is in the business of making thingamabobs. For each unit they buy material, say raw steel for $10, hire people, at a cost $1

---

[10] Google Finance at http://finance.google.com is one place to look up historical prices.

for the few minutes of assembly each thingamabob needs, and that together makes a product that sells for $15. They make $4 on every thingamabob that they sell. If they sell 100,000 thingamabobs a year, then they stand to make $400,000 in a year. How much would you pay for the business? You might say that well, if you can make 1% in your bank account, and 4% by lending out money to a government or quality business, then you might demand at least a 10% return on your money for the extra risk of owning this business. So if you bought Company X for $4 million then their yearly $400,000 in profit would be that 10% return. You then just divide by the number of shares[11] to get the price you might be willing to pay per share.

Except then you have to realize that the $400,000 might be what they made *last year*. As an investor, you have to concern yourself with the long-term future of the company: what will they make next year, and the year after, and so on? Maybe you think thingamabobs will surge in popularity and they'll sell more in the future. Then you might be willing to pay even more than $4M for the business. Or perhaps a news story just announced that raw steel prices were going up along with labour costs, and now you're afraid they may not make any money selling thingamabobs so you wouldn't buy Company X at any price.

Then consider that you're not the only one trying to come up with this value, that the information flow is changing almost daily, that the return from competing investments fluctuates, and that people get emotional (by turns greedy and fearful) and you can quickly see where the volatility in the stock market comes from. Though I believe it is *possible* to determine the fair intrinsic value of

---

[11] The number of shares is arbitrary: you could split a business up into just two shares, or into millions of equal pieces.

a company, it is not an easy pursuit. Remember that there are scores of very smart people whose entire job is to determine the prices of stocks. Will you be able to better judge what price is fair?

If you're a beginner and reading this book then I would say that no, it is not something you want to attempt. **Fortunately, you don't have to**.

What if, instead of trying to buy shares in one company and hope that you get it right, instead you bought a small piece of *all* of them? Or, at least, a great many of them. Then as long as companies in general continue to grow and make profits (as they have for hundreds of years), you should share in a portion of that and come out all right, without any need for in-depth analysis or the ability to out-think all the other analysts valuing companies. You can, with something as simple as a mutual fund.

Mutual Funds

Stocks are risky. Any single one can perform poorly, right up to the point of becoming totally worthless. Or, they could be brilliant, turning a small initial investment into a fabulous fortune as the decades pass[12]. Determining *in advance* which is which can be tough, indeed, an endeavour so unlikely to succeed that many people recommend not to bother attempting the analysis in the first place. Many professionals get paid huge salaries to play this game, and yet their aggregate average track records are simply not inspiring.

And because of the risk you absolutely do not want to have all of your eggs in one basket. **Diversification** then becomes a very important thing: spreading out your investments to different companies. And not just separate but related companies: you want to diversify between sectors[13] and in the companies of different countries[14].

Fortunately, diversification is easy with a mutual fund: a fund is just a collection of things you can invest in, bonds or stocks or a mixture of both.

---

[12] Some examples: Ford stock has increased a scant 30% over the last two decades, though it also paid a dividend through much of that time. GM stock became worthless when it went bankrupt in 2009. Toyota increased 4-fold. Magna, which makes car parts, increased nearly 10-fold.

[13] "Sectors" being how we classify businesses together: banks might be one sector, retail another, resource extraction a third, etc.

[14] This is particularly important for Canadian investors, as Canada is but a small part of the world economy, and our economy is not diversified across very many sectors.

There are many different kinds of mutual funds out there, and some are better than others. The typical mutual fund in Canada is not necessarily an ideal investment because of fees: they charge on average[15] over 2.4% per year (as their MER). Many will promise you higher returns (or safer returns) in their advertising material. However, the vast majority do not produce enough extra returns versus an index to justify the fees they charge.

An **index** is simply a large well-diversified collection of stocks or bonds. Indexes can be thought of as a way to provide the average return of the stock market by collecting many or all of the companies available. They also serve as a baseline for funds to compare themselves against.

There are five main indexes to be aware of:

The TSX composite index consists of approximately 300 companies traded on the Toronto Stock Exchange. Most are Canadian companies, though many have operations in the US and overseas as well. There is a concentration of companies in the resource and financial sectors, due to the makeup of the companies on the Toronto Stock Exchange, but there is a pretty good amount of diversification present.

The S&P 500 consists of approximately 500 companies traded in the US. Many are giant international conglomerates, and it's well-balanced across many economic sectors. This is one of the most followed indexes in the world.

---

[15] Morningstar puts the average Canadian equity mutual fund at 2.42% for 2013. Canada is the only country to get an "F" for fees in the report. *Global Fund Investor Experience 2013 Report.* http://corporate.morningstar.com/us/documents/Methodology Documents/FactSheets/Global-Fund-Investor-Experience-Report-2013.pdf

The Dow Jones Industrial Average is a smaller index of 30 US companies. It's not nearly as well diversified as the S&P 500, and the method of averaging is different, but it is one of the very first stock market indexes so it has a lot of history and remains popular. Despite the smaller number of names, it correlates well with the broader S&P 500. I would recommend just sticking with the S&P 500 for US stocks.

The MSCI EAFE (Europe, Australia, Far East) index tracks several European markets and developed nations markets around the world (e.g. Japan and Australia). This is the main "international/rest of the world" index for Canadians to follow.

The FTSE TMX Canada Universe bond index is a broadly diversified set of bonds, with about 70% government bonds and 30% investment-grade corporate bonds (that is, bonds from companies with high credit ratings).

As I mentioned earlier, most mutual funds will have some strategy to try to do better than just simply following one of these indexes (or "benchmarks"). However, with their high fees they very often fall short. To be sure, *some* do beat the indexes. The problem is, it's nearly impossible to know *in advance* which funds will be the ones to do well.

Passive Investing

Fortunately there is a strategy for those who accept that it is difficult to beat an index after paying fees: **passive investing**[16]. With passive investing one simply accepts that trying to do better than the index doesn't usually work, and that the average return is good enough. Instead of trying to pick the best stocks, which is difficult (perhaps impossible) to control, you just invest in the index itself. Though indexes started as theoretical ways to benchmark investors – an average yardstick to compare against – index funds were created so that you could invest directly in an index. These funds simply hold the whole collection of stocks or bonds that are represented in the index. Instead of trying to find winning stocks to get the best return – and failing, more often than not – the focus of index funds on reducing your fees, which unlike returns *is* something that can be controlled.

There are mutual funds that follow this passive investing strategy, with the main features being low fees. The two best index fund options in the Canadian marketplace – based on the measures of low fees and ease-of-use for a novice investor – are TD Canada Trust's e-series mutual funds and Tangerine's Investment Funds (formerly ING Streetwise). These options will be discussed in detail in the *Putting It Into Practice* section.

There are also things called **Exchange-Traded Funds (ETFs)**: these are mutual funds that you buy and sell on a stock exchange like a stock. They feature even lower annual MERs, but you have to pay commissions to buy

---

[16] Sometimes called index investing, or a "couch potato" approach.

and sell[17]. The math to figure out when it's better to go with a regular index mutual fund (with higher MERs but no transaction fees) or an ETF is not too hard to do on your own, but the shortcut answer is above about $50,000 in assets it makes sense to put in the extra effort (and pay the commissions) to use ETFs if you're with a typical big-bank brokerage. With commission-free ETF providers (like Questrade) it makes financial sense to use ETFs right from your first investment, though to avoid account fees you should have at least $5,000 ready. For the added complication involved you may wish to have a more than that to invest – depending on how onerous you find the extra work to use ETFs.

---

[17] Though several brokerages now offer a menu of ETFs commission-free, at least to buy, including Questrade which will be covered in depth later.

Mutual Funds vs. Index Funds vs. ETFs

	Regular Mutual Funds	Index Funds	ETFs
Account	Can be purchased from a simple mutual funds account or select brokerage accounts; managed account or self-directed	Can be purchased from a simple mutual funds account or select brokerage accounts; usually self-directed accounts only	Can be purchased from any brokerage account – even funds trading on US exchanges can be purchased; usually self-directed accounts only
Fees/MERs	Typically the highest in the world, over 2%/year. Usually no fee to buy, but can have deferred sales charges (DSC) to sell early (and "early" can mean up to 7 years)	Usually no fees to purchase or sell; middle-range ongoing fees of ~1% for many index funds, but <0.5% for TD e-series	Commissions to sell, usually commission to buy, depending on the brokerage. Lowest ongoing fees
Minimum Holding Period	Usually a minimum holding period, can be extremely long (up to 7 years)	Usually a minimum holding period (none for Tangerine, 30 days for TD e-series, both discussed later)	No minimum holding period
Selection	Vast array available	Somewhat limited, major indexes with perhaps some currency neutral options	Vast array available, not all are *passive index* ETFs, like with mutual funds
Pricing	Based on value of underlying holdings	Based on value of underlying holdings	Based on market trading, *usually* tied very closely to value of underlying holdings
Units	Can buy partial units to invest to the last penny	Can buy partial units to invest to the last penny	Must purchase whole units, preferably in blocks of 100 units
Minimum Investment	Usually $100 to both open an account and make an individual purchase; pre-authorized purchases can be set up for as little as $25 per purchase	Usually $100 to both open an account and make an individual purchase; pre-authorized purchases can be set up for as little as $25 per purchase (even less through Tangerine)	Usually $5,000 - $15,000 to avoid fees on account; minimum individual purchase depends on ETF value and when it makes sense to pay a commission (if applicable)

The idea is to then get a return that's *good enough*, with only as many risks as you're willing to accept, while minimizing your fees. Since the market as a whole can be thought of as the average of all the mutual funds' trading activity, by going with an index approach you'll get the average return. But because your fees will be lower than the average fund, you'll actually do *better* than the average *investor* in those funds.

Passive investing involves minimizing fees while buying broadly-diversified funds holding stocks and bonds that track **indexes**. The main **index funds** to keep in mind are:

- A bond fund (like one that follows the DEX Universe Index)

- A Canadian stock fund (like one that follows the S&P TSX Composite Index)

- A US stock fund (like one that follows the S&P 500 Index)

- An international stock fund (like one that follows the MSCI EAFE Index).

These funds can either be traditional mutual funds, or funds traded on a stock exchange (**ETFs**).

Risk and Historical Returns

I mentioned earlier that stocks are risky because they can and do occasionally give poor returns, including going right to zero. They don't *all* go to zero though, so with diversification even if a few perform poorly, the overall average will still do well in the long term. Indeed, history tells us that the best long-term returns are available from investing in a collection of stocks across many industries and countries. Though they can be very volatile, particularly in the short term, over time the volatility has a way of working itself out.

In the short term the market as a whole (or an index representing it) can go down 50% or more. As you give the market more and more time to work out the short-term fluctuations stocks become less risky[18]. For holding periods of longer than 20 years the market has never been down[19].

---

[18] Less risky in the common-sense understanding of the chance of permanently destroying your capital; the volatility in terms of the spread between your best-case and worst-case scenarios gets bigger over time though.

[19] A few asterisks have to be used with "never" – the best data is for the US market. There are a few counter-examples (for example, investing in Japanese stocks just before their crash in the late 80's), but they're rare enough that the point stands: in the long run, the volatility works itself out and stocks are a good investment.

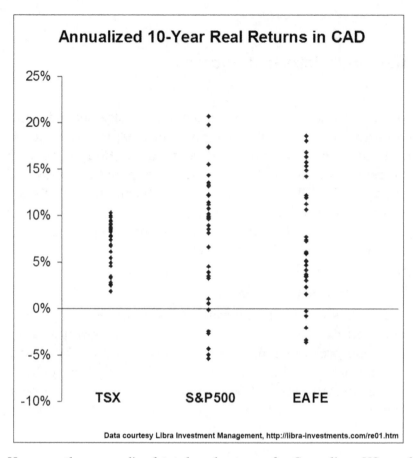

Here are the annualized total real returns for Canadian, US, and
international equities over rolling ten-year periods – that is, this
chart shows you the average return you would get each year
through the ten-year periods of 1970-1979, 1971-1980, 1972-
1981, etc., through to 2004-2013. The returns have been
adjusted back to Canadian dollars, adjusted for inflation, and
include dividends. Note that all of the negative returns in this
data include the 2008/2009 market crash, but not all ten-year
periods that include the crash had negative returns. Source data
collected and provided by Libra Investment Management,
libra-investments.com/re01.htm.

For some history, there have been quite a number of
market crashes where stocks declined. The worst was the
1929 crash that marked the beginning of the Great

Depression. Stocks fell some 90% and took about 25 years to recover[20]. But recover they did, and if you would allow yourself to mark that experience down as a one-off, never-to-be-repeated event, then the worst market crashes involve stocks declining by about 50% (including the recent 2008-2009 market crash). Though those events can be quite painful for investors at the time, they do pass and the markets go on to set new highs. If you held on after any given crash the prices recovered within a few years – that's long enough that in your day-to-day life you'd wonder if the prices would ever recover, but short enough that it *would* happen soon enough to matter.

The long-term average real return has been about 6-7% from American stock returns (Canadian are *similar*, but American stocks are the best studied). That includes dividends, and is after inflation (hence the "real" return). More on the importance of inflation in a few pages.

When deciding whether to invest in equities, and how much you can allocate to them, on top of your time horizon is the matter of **risk tolerance**: your ability to receive a statement from your financial institution showing that the value of your investments had been cut in half, and to not panic or lose sleep at night – or worse yet, log in to your account and sell all of your holdings out of fear or disgust. If you're the type of person who would panic in the midst of prices falling, seeing everyone else selling and decide that you would join the pack, you would take a "paper loss"[21] that might recover (and given the historical record, would in all likelihood do so) and transform it into a permanent loss. Better in that case to stick to safer investments right from the beginning. Better

---

[20] This time, not including dividends.

[21] A paper loss is when your stocks or mutual funds decrease in value from what you paid for them, but you still own the same number of units. When you sell, you turn it into a *realized* loss.

still though to separate emotions from your investing, and keep a coldly rational long-term perspective.

You need to sort out your risk tolerance in advance: the midst of a market panic and sell-off is not the time to discover your risk tolerance isn't what you thought and to try to change your plan when it is most expensive to do so. Indeed, that is the time to pull out your planning binder and remind yourself of the long-term plan and what you decided you should do in a market downturn when you were in a calm and rational state.

Unfortunately, there isn't much of a substitute for that real-world experience of living through a market crash. In Frank Herbert's science fiction masterpiece *Dune*, a young Paul Atreides had to endure a test of his humanity, wherein a magical box simulated the experience of excruciating pain (but left no lasting tissue damage); he had to display the ability to withstand short-term pain in the interest of his long-term future by holding his hand in the box and enduring it by sheer force of will. There are times I wish a similar test existed for investors to accurately gauge their risk tolerance before a market crash. Instead you will just have to make the most honest assessment of yourself that you can, and attempt to prepare yourself for what may come.

Note though that risk tolerance can also include things like your job or life situation: if you're in a field that is very boom-and-bust, then you may not want to invest as much in stocks which can also be boom-and-bust-like, because you may find yourself unemployed at the same time that the investments you'll need to live off of are selling for less. If you're younger, you have more time to wait for a market recovery or adjust your savings plan than if you are close to retirement. The young can also be more certain of their continued ability to work and save, whereas when you get older your chance of having your investment timeline cut short by a chronic disease increase.

Risk tolerance also touches on your financial ability to suffer losses without destroying your life. If you have a large financial cushion or flexibility in your financial needs you may have a higher risk tolerance. For example, if you were planning on buying a car in four years that would generally be considered too short a time-frame to risk putting the money you have saved up in equities. Yet if you had the flexibility to buy a *cheaper* car *if* you *did* suffer a loss, or to delay your purchase by a few years, it might not be such a black-and-white situation as the timeline alone suggests.

Though I have attempted to put you into the proper mindset with all the warnings of the riskiness of stocks, the simple fact is that investing in stocks is the only easily accessible way to get such high expected returns, with so little effort and expertise required. The warnings are to prepare you for the inevitable rough ride in investing, and not to scare you off of investing entirely. Indeed, including at least some exposure to stocks is critical to reducing your overall risk of running out of money in retirement.

Keep in mind that the volatility of the stock market is very attention-grabbing; market crashes are stressful times and stories of hardship and loss can get passed down through the generations. However, the hidden risks of paying too much in fees or starting too late can be just as costly over the long run – and you cannot recover from those by waiting.

And though I would caution against trying to "time the market", better returns come from buying when the market is low (remember the aphorism "buy low, sell high"). That will bring us to rebalancing later, but it's important to remember that when you're in the phase of your life when you're saving money (i.e. when you're young), you want to be buying stocks when they're cheaper. So if (*when*) a market crash comes along, that's not the time to wring your hands, lament your losses, and consider selling and getting out of the crazy world of investing. Instead it's the time to cheer the bargains, to buy more, to take advantage of the temporary insanity of the traders to set yourself up for later. Market crashes, as much as they are feared and vilified in the media, usually end up being good for a young investor, and conversely, people do not make money by "waiting for things to settle down." As long as you have faith that in the long term businesses will continue to be profitable and grow, then eventually your diversified investments should perform for you.

> Understanding your **risk tolerance** in advance is critical for investing success and your ability to stick to your plan through future volatility. Risk tolerance has many components, including details of your situation as well as your psychology.
>
> In the short term, equities can have large losses and high volatility. But history shows that patient investors have been well rewarded over the long term.

Tax

Canadians are well acquainted with the concept of taxation. Like money you earn from a job, income you earn from investing is taxable, however, investments are not all taxed the same. I will note that many Canadians will be able to keep all of their investments within a tax shelter (discussed in the next chapters), and won't have to worry about the taxes in this chapter.

Interest income, like from a savings account, GIC, or bond is fully taxed, which means that you pay tax on the income from the interest at your full marginal rate[22].

To encourage people to take some risks with their money – which is important for investments in business and the functioning of the economy – the government doesn't tax gains from investments in stocks as much as they do safe investments.

Capital gains, what happens when you buy something and sell it for more, are only taxed at half the rate of regular income. You also don't pay any capital gains tax until you actually sell[23] your shares, so if you're a long-

---

[22]There are common misunderstandings of how tax brackets work – they can be confusing. The tax rate is just applied on the "marginal" dollars in that bracket. It is not possible to make more money pre-tax and end up with less after-tax from a raise or investment moving you "up a tax bracket" – only that last extra bit is taxed at the higher rate. For more, see *Advanced Tax* on page 158.

[23] There is something called a *deemed disposition* where you could have to pay capital gains tax even without selling. The most common case would be if you owned something in a regular account, then moved it into a registered account like an

term holder of a stock (or index fund that holds stocks) you can put off having to pay any tax for a long time. If you have any capital losses they count against your capital gains, so you only pay tax on your *net* gain. If you end up with a net loss for the year, you can carry it forward to count against future capital gains, or even revise your tax returns for up to three years in the past and apply the losses.

Dividends are paid out from the earnings of a company to shareholders. The company has already paid tax on those earnings, so a tax credit is provided to the investor to account for the double taxation. The formula is a little complex, but the end result is that dividends are one of the most tax-efficient forms of regular income you'll find. An important caveat to that is that dividends generate income that gets taxed every year, whereas capital gains can be deferred. Also, if you have any income-tested government benefits such as the Guaranteed Income Supplement, then dividends can be undesirable because a greater amount is added to the income figure used in the test for eligibility. Called the dividend "gross-up" it's a strange concept, but your tax software will handle all the calculations for you. Briefly, it's as though the government pretends that *you* made all the money the corporation did to pay out the dividend in the first place, then gives you a tax credit to make up for the taxes the corporation paid.

If you own a mutual fund, the fund company or your brokerage will send you a form for income taxes (called a T3) in the spring of each year, making it easy to report your interest and dividend income. They may also report some capital gains on that form, which you must claim. These capital gains however come from the individual

---

RRSP – even though you didn't actually sell, it did leave your taxable account.

stocks within the fund being bought and sold. You still need to keep track of what you paid for the fund, and then what you eventually sell it for so that you can report the *overall* capital gains/losses from owning the fund. This will be covered in more detail in the *Record Keeping* section on page 128.

Return-of-capital is the last type of payment you may receive from an investment. This will eventually count as a capital gain, except you get the payment now. You will pay the tax later because return-of-capital reduces your average cost – for example, if you paid $5 per share for a company or mutual fund, and received $1 in return-of-capital, well in tax terms that's just your own money coming back to you. So now you have $1 in cash, and a share that now has a cost of $4. If you sell at $5, you have a $1 taxable capital gain. It's a little cumbersome to track, as you must record it yourself each year until you sell the investment (you will get a tax slip – a T3 – from your brokerage detailing the return of capital for any investments).

This is all assuming that you are keeping your investments in a regular taxable account (also known as "non-registered"). To encourage long-term savings the government also has several registered accounts that can reduce the taxes on investing and also the bookkeeping required. The next three sections will detail the most commonly used registered accounts: the TFSA, RRSP, and RESP. Many Canadians will be able to keep *all* of their investments in their registered accounts.

One important thing to remember for all these accounts is that you put investments (or cash) inside them, you don't "buy an RRSP". They're baskets, not fruits. You can hold pretty much the whole range of investments you would hold outside these accounts: cash, GICs, bonds, stocks, and mutual funds made up of combinations of the above.

TFSA – Tax-Free Savings Account

This is the newest registered account type and is the simplest to understand: investments you put in this account are not taxed. You simply put in money to buy an investment (or just keep it in cash and earn interest), and there's no tax on any gains, whether those are dividends, capital gains, or interest[24]. You can withdraw as much as you want from the account with no penalties, though the bank or brokerage that hosts the account for you may charge a withdrawal fee.

You get a certain amount of TFSA **contribution room** per year: right now (2017) that's $5500 per year, but that will be increased by the government periodically to account for inflation. Whether you use it or not, your contribution room is increasing every year from when you turn 18. So if you were 18 or older when the TFSA was introduced in 2009, you have (as of 2017) $52,000 of room ($5000 from each of 2009, 2010, 2011 and 2012 and $5500 from 2013, 2014, 2016, and 2017, with $10,000 from 2015). You get that room on January 1 of each year, so it makes sense to make your contributions early if you can.

If you make any withdrawals through the year from your TFSA, you get that amount added back to your contribution room the **following** year. That makes the TFSA a really flexible account, because you can use it for

---

[24] Note that foreign governments don't necessarily recognize the tax-free nature of TFSAs so dividends from US investments may lead to some withholding tax from those governments that would not occur in an RRSP. This will be discussed more in *A Twist: US ETFs* on page 152.

long-term tax-free investing, but you also have the option of withdrawing without permanently losing the room if you suddenly find yourself in need of the money.

While you have your money in the TFSA, it doesn't matter what happens to your investments: you can trade them around or just sit in cash. You can make obscene amounts of money with a hot stock, or lose it all in a poor investment. None of that will affect your contribution room: only what you put into the account from outside and what you take back out from within the confines of the TFSA to the outside matters.

Think of the TFSA like rabbits in your backyard. Your parents at the front door are the government. They say you can bring 5 bunnies into the backyard every year. Beyond that, they're looking out at the front door, so they don't care what happens in the backyard.

You can have your bunnies reproduce like, well, bunnies; you can put them all in one big pen or a bunch of different ones. It doesn't matter, as long as no more than five bunnies go past your parents per year on the way in.

If you need to take a bunny out for some reason, like to bring it to show and tell at school, your parents will remember you took that bunny out and will let you put it back in the *next* calendar year without counting it against your limit of five bunnies per year – it's not a *new* bunny (i.e. the ability to re-contribute withdrawals). Even if you did really well at bunny farming and want to bring all 40 of your bunnies to school with you, your parents will count them up and let you bring those back in the next year in addition to your new year's limit of 5 bunnies. And if you didn't collect any bunnies one year, you can collect 10 in the year after.

If you don't handle your bunnies well and they all die, your parents don't want to hear about it; you can't bring in any more bunnies (i.e. if you lose money, you don't get the contribution room back – it's *contributions* that matter, *not account balance*). Contrarily, if you withdraw and contribute multiple times in the same year you can over-contribute, even if the balance at any one time never went over your limit – it's only money *going in* within a single year that counts to your contribution room, and the money coming out is only tallied up for the following year's contribution room.

Finally, the contribution room is by calendar year. You can contribute your full limit on December 10th, take it out December 29th, and put it back in on January 2nd the following calendar year and not over-contribute – indeed, you'd have $5,500 more room – even though less than a week went by. But if you take it out January 2nd instead, you can't put it back until the following year.

A lot of people try to over-think the TFSA. It's really not that complicated, and no, there aren't any loopholes to exploit in terms of moving money in and out and keeping your contribution room, or from over-contributing. Though the Canada Revenue Agency will run through the figures to see how much contribution room you have for your TFSA to charge penalties if you go over, they are consistently behind the times with this calculation so you can't rely on the numbers in your statements or on their web portal to know how much you have to contribute. The banks and brokerages will not stop you from over-contributing. You need to track your contributions yourself.

Focus on the year-to-year contribution room. Every January 1, your contribution room becomes your old room, plus the new room every Canadian gets (currently $5,500 each year, for 2017), plus any withdrawals made in the previous year. Then, for the purposes of how much room you have in the tax shelter, you can ignore what happens within it.

RRSP – Registered Retirement Savings Plan

An RRSP[25] is a bit more complicated than a TFSA.

For the RRSP, you put in "pre-tax" money – that is, any money you put in you are not taxed on, so you get a tax deduction to use. Investments within it are able to grow and compound tax-free, and it frees you from some paperwork and reporting burden, just like the TFSA.

Your contribution room for an RRSP is not as simple as the TFSA. You get a certain amount of your income for each year as RRSP contribution room, up to a maximum per year, with an adjustment if you have a pension. To make it easy, the Canada Revenue Agency will calculate your RRSP contribution room and report it on your annual statement of account. The option to contribute and get a deduction for a given year continues for the 60 days into the next year, often called "RRSP season".

When it comes time to take money out of the RRSP it is then taxed as ordinary income. You also don't get the contribution room back (except for a few specific programs that allow you to borrow from your RRSP to buy a house or go to school)[26]. This means that you really should be sure you don't need access to money in your RRSP until retirement. It also means that in a certain sense not all of the money in an RRSP is yours: some of it

---

[25] Often just called RSP, especially by the banks (they seem prone to dropping an R).

[26] Note that you have to make the withdrawal through the program – your bank will have a special form for requesting a withdrawal through the Home Buyer's Plan (HBP) or Lifelong Learning Plan (LLP) – you can't just simply transfer money out of your RSP.

can be thought of as the government's portion that they will get back when you withdraw. So when comparing the RRSP and TFSA, you have to remember that you need to put *more* in the RRSP for the situations to be truly comparable, to account for the government's portion.

The "no tax on contribution but tax on withdrawal" aspect makes the RRSP ideal for situations where you expect to be taxed less when you take the money out than you were when you put the money in. For most people that *is* the case when they're saving while working and withdrawing when they retire. Other situations where you earn less can be good fits for the RRSP too, like withdrawing while on a break from work, whether that's for an extended period of unemployment, a sabbatical, maternity leave, or going back to school. In the particular case of going back to school there is also the Lifelong Learning Plan (LLP), which lets you temporarily withdraw funds without losing contribution room or paying tax, with the requirement that you repay them on a set schedule.

A further complication of having withdrawals count as income is that taking money out of your RRSP could reduce the income-tested benefits you receive such as Old Age Security (OAS) or the Guaranteed Income Supplement (GIS), increasing your effective tax rate in retirement.

As to which account is better, the RRSP or the TFSA, that depends a bit on the person and their situation, but in general the TFSA is better for people in lower tax brackets[27] (and because those people make less, $5,500/year in savings might be all they have) while the RRSP is better for those in higher tax brackets, or who expect to be in a lower tax bracket come withdrawal time.

---

[27] Roughly speaking, a low tax bracket would refer to someone making less than $40k/year.

A simple rule-of-thumb[28] is that the **TFSA room should be used first.** The RRSP may end up being the most advantageous for some people, but the TFSA is more flexible if you need access to your savings in an emergency. Or, if you're just starting out you may decide that you don't like the bank or brokerage you chose. Whatever the reason, withdrawing from the TFSA, waiting until the next calendar year, and starting over is a nice option to have.

Moreover, the math that finds RRSPs are better for some situations in head-to-head comparisons assumes that the tax refund you get *is also invested* (or you take out a loan to put more in the RRSP in the first place, and pay it off with the refund). Many people, however, have a certain amount of cash in their chequing accounts and contribute that at the end of the month or year, and then their tax refund ends up being spent – becoming a vacation or big-screen TV instead of more RRSP investments. In that case the TFSA is the better choice as it doesn't tempt you into squandering a big part of your investment. And those in higher tax brackets where RRSPs are the clear winner will likely find that they have enough money to max out their TFSA *and* still put a large chunk into their RRSP anyway. Plus, in general TFSA accounts are largely without annual fees, no matter the size of the account, whereas some RRSP providers do charge annual fees for smaller accounts.

The big caveat to my TFSA-first advice is that you need to have the willpower to leave the investments in the TFSA unless you absolutely need them. If you can't be trusted with yourself and need to lock your money away so it's even harder to get at, then the RRSP is the better option.

---

[28] Individual circumstances vary. If you are lucky enough to have a job that provides matching RRSP contributions, then use that first: free money trumps tax considerations every time.

Also, some employers offer to match your RRSP contributions which should be taken first – it's free money! See http://www.holypotato.net/?p=1403 for a TFSA vs RRSP decision guide.

RESP – Registered Education Savings Plan

There are two big advantages to opening a RESP for a child: the first is that any investment gains in the account will be taxed in the hands of the child if they go to college or university. And since college kids generally don't have much income and lots of tuition tax credits, that income ends up being basically tax-free. The other huge benefit is that the federal government will provide grants[29] to boost your contribution to the plan: a 20% match for your contributions up to $2,500 per year (i.e., $500 from the government if you put in $2,500).

Low-income parents should also consider setting up a RESP and investing a small amount, despite the hardship, because there are bonus grants[30] to help give their children a chance. Even contributing a few thousand over several years while a child is young will help keep them eligible for grants in their late teens, when they might contribute to their own RESPs from summer jobs, gifts, or other savings of their own. For some low-income parents – those eligible for the National Child Benefit Supplement – the government will contribute funds to help start an RESP without any contribution required from the parents, all they have to do is open the account and apply. This is known as the *Canada Learning Bond*.

The plans are flexible, with many post-secondary education programs considered applicable, including

---

[29] Canada Education Savings Grants (CESG).

[30] Not all financial institutions can handle all the extended grants; the Alberta and Saskatchewan provincial ones in particular are not widely available, see this site for a full listing: www.esdc.gc.ca/en/student_loans/resp/promoters_list.page

traditional university programs, college diploma programs, trade schools, or even many apprenticeships. If the child doesn't go to university or other post-secondary education, then all the investment gains are taxed in the hands of the parents at once with a penalty, and the government grants are given back. The penalty is a 20% tax on top of your regular tax rate, which is not so severe given that you may have benefited from a decade of tax-free growth; the penalty can be side-stepped by transferring the RESP funds into your RRSP. Plans can also last a long time – up to 36 years – so even if your child doesn't go straight to university from high school, the RESP could still be useful if they choose to enroll later.

When trying to prioritize whether you should contribute to an RESP for your child against contributing to your own TFSA and RRSP, it will depend firstly on how you feel about supporting your children through post-secondary education versus balancing your own savings needs. In terms of returns, for at least the first $2,500 contributed in a year the instant 20% match from the government's CESG is very hard to beat. Beyond that, contributing more to an RESP may still be beneficial, but if you are not sure your child will need that much for school then a TFSA will be more flexible and perhaps a better choice than maxing out an RESP (the RESP has a lifetime contribution limit of $50,000).

Most students will at least *enroll* in a post-secondary education program – which is all that needs to happen to make an eligible withdrawal from an RESP – even if they don't finish with a degree, so I would not recommend basing your decision on a bet that your child may decide not to attend at all.

Different types of income are taxed in different ways. The tax considerations can be important when it comes to where to keep which investments, and in comparing the after-tax performance of different investments.

- Interest income (from savings accounts, GICs, or bonds) is taxed at your full rate, just like income from working a job.

- Capital gains (from stocks increasing in value) are taxed at half the regular rate, and are deferred until you sell.

- Dividends (from stocks) have a more complicated formula, but are taxed very favourably.

Income from investments can be sheltered in accounts like the TFSA and the RRSP. These are "baskets" not "fruits" – you buy a GIC, bond, or stock and put it *in* your TFSA or RRSP, you don't "buy an RRSP."

- The TFSA has no tax on withdrawals, but no tax deduction on contributions. You can put any amount withdrawn back in the following year, so it's best for long-term savings that *may* need to be withdrawn in the near future.

- The RRSP gives a tax deduction on contributions, but withdrawals are taxed like income. It's best for truly long-term investments.

Inflation

Inflation is the increase in the price of things over time (or expressed the other way around, the value of a dollar decreasing relative to real things over time). It's not totally uniform: though inflation has averaged 2-3% over the last few years, I've found that the price of a can of pop at my local convenience store jumped from $1 to $1.29 without hitting all the numbers in-between. The price of gas has doubled, while the price of a new computer has dropped in half in about the last 10 years. But overall, across most of the things that we buy, there has been inflation: stuff costs more.

If you have some money and you just hold on to it for a period of time, like putting it under your mattress, it ends up buying less in the future. For instance, the $100 in your sock drawer bought 100 sticks of gum when you put it there last year, but now might only buy 97 sticks. **Inflation acts like a negative return on your money**.

Similarly, even if you're earning 3% interest in a savings account, if inflation is also 3% you're only just keeping pace – that's a 0% **real return** (real here referring to after-inflation: what you can actually buy with your money). Of course, it gets worse with taxes because you pay tax on *nominal* gains: even though that savings account interest rate might just be keeping pace with inflation so you're not increasing your buying power, you will have to pay tax on the interest anyway.

In the short term, inflation is hard to notice, and not a large factor: it's more important to have the safety of a savings account for money you'll need to pay for your vacation in 6 months than it is to worry about the effects of inflation over that time. But in the long term inflation can take a real bite, and so it's important to invest in things that have a good chance of earning more than inflation is eating away.

> Inflation acts like a hidden tax on your savings, making the price of future goods higher, so your future dollars buy less. **Nominal returns** do not account for inflation, but **real returns** do.

Planning

It's important to come up with a plan to guide your financial life. There are many factors to consider, including:

- Your priorities in life
- How much you should save
- Your return on investment
- How much you'll need to spend per year in retirement
- Your timelines (how long you have to save/invest, how long you have to support yourself after)
- Other goals

Investing is just going to be a small part of that overall plan, but will be important in helping you to reach your long-term goals. The plan will also help you figure out how much you can spend and save, when you will need it, and how much risk you can take along the way.

Planning is in a way a giant balancing act, where you will try to save enough to have the investments you need to support yourself in retirement, but not scrimp so much that you overly sacrifice today's quality-of-life and enjoyment.

Be sure to be realistic, as it does no good to come up with a plan that won't even come close to playing out in real life: as easy as retirement saving looks with a 20%/year return plugged into your spreadsheet, it's not going to happen.

There's a whole profession of financial planners out there with their own professional designation (CFP) with a host of detailed, complicated software tools that can account for different investment returns, inflation, taxes, etc. When you get closer to retirement (within a decade or two) then it may very well be worth paying a visit to one to draw up a detailed plan. But if you're younger (20's and 30's) then the uncertainty of the future is so great that the details probably aren't all that important: you can get close enough by yourself with a few minutes of careful thought and a spreadsheet.

Just try to save as much as you can get away with early on, invest it wisely, and you'll set yourself up to be in fine shape by the time you're at the point where the details will matter enough to make it worth paying to have a professional look at your situation.

For each component of your plan be sure to consider a range: what if returns were 4%? 5%, 6%, 7%, 8%? Your plan shouldn't be a single number and single, straightforward route planned through your life: you should be prepared for the inevitable detours and bumps in the road. Indeed, I highly recommend printing your plan out in hard copy with notes to your future self (like: "market crashes always feel terrifying when you're in the middle of them, but just hang on and don't sell now – the plan is to rebalance!")[31].

-----

[31] Rebalancing will be covered in just a few more sections on page 69.

John Robertson

The Cone of Probability

Here is how many people plan for retirement (and many similar activities that involve projections): come up with reasonable estimates of the relevant parameters. Plug them into an online calculator or spreadsheet to do the math. Have a cookie.

Yet you really can't just say that the average investment return is 6%, your average spending needs are $40,000/year, inflation will be 2%, plug that all into a spreadsheet and call your financial planning exercise completed. That might be your expected, *most likely* outcome and an excellent *start*. You can plot it for a nice, smooth exponential growth trajectory that can make for a very comforting graph.

While your future might have a good chance of looking *something* like that, it's highly unlikely to be *precisely* like that. I am very suspicious of false precision. There's a whole range of possible outcomes. So to start with I'd add a "best case" and "worst case" projection, to get something like this:

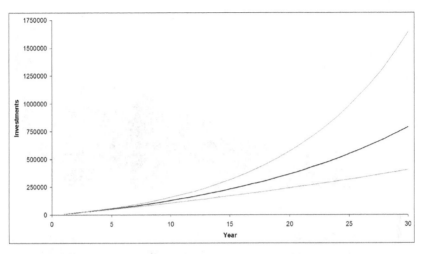

Savings and investments plotted over 30 years with a most likely or "base" case of 6% investment returns, along with best case (10%) and worst case (2%) scenarios.

Now you have some idea of the range of future outcomes, and may even be able to say how those might compare to what you're willing to accept, and use this to set some limits and guidelines for your future course corrections. Maybe if by year 5 you're closer to the bottom worst-case track than the middle most-likely one, you'll increase your savings rate to compensate. But even that is not really capturing the uncertainty and more importantly the variability ahead. There's a big *cloud of probability* around the outcomes, and this is just a small, simplified part of a projection to retirement.

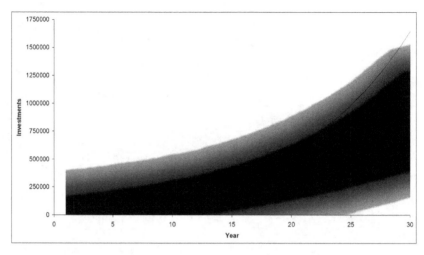

A visualization of a cloud of probability – of uncertainty – around potential future outcomes. The cloud is an artists' rendition and not a statistical display or calculation.

Because the future is so inherently uncertain, I generally tell people with a lot of future ahead of them to not sweat the fine details: tweaking your asset allocation to the last half a percent really won't matter when you can only guess at future returns to plus or minus 5%/yr, and even then only over longer periods of time. Indeed, my training as a scientist has given me an appreciation for the inherent uncertainty in everything.

That's a tough, uncomfortable concept for many. *"We demand rigidly defined areas of doubt and uncertainty!"*[32] The unknown is scary and weird, and uncertainty looks a lot like the unknown with math thrown on top. As terrifying as this is going to sound, you can't hide from uncertainty.

Control what you can – keep fees low, save a decent amount of your income, start early, don't panic – and be

---

[32] Douglas Adams, *The Hitchhiker's Guide to the Galaxy*

prepared to be surprised and make adjustments on the rest. Get started in approximately the right direction, try to keep moving in the right direction through an iterative process of small course corrections, and try not to fear the uncertainty. The future will – at best – only look approximately like how we imagine it will. That uncertainty is just a fact of life.

I've created a spreadsheet to help you estimate how much you may need to save based on a best, base, and worst-case scenario approach, and also how long your investments may last into retirement based on your current savings rate. The spreadsheet, whimsically named the Ballparkinator, and a more detailed description are available at www.holypotato.net/?p=1243. Note that the spreadsheet is not a full financial plan – even just for estimating a ballpark for your savings rate it only considers retirement and not other savings goals like for a car, vacation, child's education, or house down-payment.

On Course Corrections

There is uncertainty in the world. This makes many people deeply uncomfortable, but the facts are inescapable. The solution is not to pretend that the uncertainty is not there, but to prepare for it. That means that any plan you create – no matter how good – is not going to end up playing out perfectly. You will have to make adjustments as you go. However, not every deviation from the plan is worth worrying about and trying to correct.

Let's think of financial planning as taking a voyage across the ocean. I appreciate that this may be a poor choice of metaphors as I am not a sailor and most likely neither are you, but let's work through it.

You set off with some destination in mind. Checking the map and detailed charts with the typical winds and currents ahead, you draw a line to plot your course (with the help of some basic high school trigonometry to factor in the wind and current). With a glance at the stars to be sure, you set your sails and put your back into the oars. The journey of a lifetime!

Within minutes you find you're off course: a particularly larger-than-average wave has just moved your bow a half-degree off course and slowed you imperceptibly. No matter, a quick calculation, a pull on the oars and an adjustment of the rudder has set you right again. Then another wave. And a gust of wind… which then suddenly dies as fast as it came on.

The conclusion is obvious: you simply can't adjust for every ripple, it would drive you mad and lead to needless effort trying to compensate for tiny effects that may just cancel themselves out anyway. But you can't very well cross an ocean without making a few course adjustments, otherwise when you do hit shore (*if* you hit shore) you may find out that you're way off target. Ending up in Bangor, Maine is way worse than ending up in Halifax as planned (have you *read* Stephen King's documentaries on the horrors plaguing Maine?). Some kind of compromise has to be reached that will let you respond to the important changes so that you can get back on course, without over-correcting to every little thing.

To leave the metaphor and talk about financial planning, for problems like this there are lots practical solutions. You could just limit how often you check to see if you're off course (e.g. once a year), or act only when you're off course by more than some threshold value[33].

Some adjustments may be more major, and require much more of an effort to correct for, like disability, losing a job, or a major global market crash. They're also usually highly emotional times, which can lead to less-than-optimal decision-making. The midst of a market crash is the last time you want to be re-evaluating your risk tolerance and end up selling low, and while you're sick and unable to work may not be the time to concentrate on reworking your financial plan. So part of the planning process should ideally involve sketching out your course corrections **in advance**.

I don't want to dictate how you prepare for and make your course adjustments, just that you do. A general scheme to prepare for the future and any course corrections might have two relatively simple components:

1. Identify – in advance – points where you will assess your progress. Decide how you will measure that

---

[33] For example, if your asset allocation – which we'll talk about in the next section – is off by more than say 5%.

progress, and what deviation would call for corrective action. What events are worth responding to, which are not?

2. Decide what action you will take while things are calm and you have your background research front of mind. **Write your contingency plans down.** You don't want to be making those decisions while emotional after realizing that your plan is not working out, or trusting a plan from years earlier to a foggy memory.

For example, if you find after five years that your savings rate has lagged (perhaps because you can't stay on budget, perhaps because of several emergencies/unemployment/etc), how would you get back on track? What would you do to your budget, how would your investments change? If equity returns were lower than planned for 10 years, would you put more into equities because you expect some mean reversion and that's part of your rebalancing, or less because they're losing and you're afraid of that trend continuing? This is one area where your answer in advance might be different than your emotional answer later.

Asset Allocation

There are a lot of ways to split up your investments and to try to strike a balance between potential returns and safety, convenience and diversification. Your **asset allocation** refers to how much money you put into which types of investments, or *asset classes*. You might want to get really detailed and decide how much to invest in bonds, and then split that up into government bonds and corporate bonds and high-yield bonds... but that's a lot of work, and going into that kind of detail may not improve your end result.

To keep it simple, I'm going to focus on the largest, easiest-to-buy components. This is also a very good compromise that should give you good returns going forward without putting yourself at risk of "over-fitting" by trying to fine-tune your allocation to dozens of sub-sectors, in amounts that ultimately are not likely to be meaningful.

Emergency fund: Some money kept in a savings account or cashable GIC that you can get to in short order if needed[34]. You can combine this with saving for specific near-term purchases (like new appliances, cars, or vacations), as long as you have a reserve for emergencies[35] like getting sick, losing your job, etc. There

---

[34] For more risk-tolerant investors you can invest your emergency fund, especially if it's for "true" emergencies and not just periodic spending. Be sure to have a buffer in that case, as you may find markets are down when you need to withdraw for an emergency.

[35] That means not draining your emergency fund for non-emergency purchases – if you have $5,000 set aside for emergencies and are also saving $10,000 for a new car in your

should be enough available to you on short notice to pay for a few months of rent/mortgage/utilities/etc. A good rule of thumb is three months of your essential living expenses: more, and you're likely being too conservative and that money could be better invested in the markets; less, and you're likely leaving yourself without a cushion.

Bonds: The more stable part of your long-term portfolio. There are lots of rules of thumb around for how much to keep in bonds: one I like is to keep a percentage equal to your age less 10 (so if you're 20, 10% should be in bonds; at 55, 45% would be in bonds). If you have less tolerance for risk, you should have more in bonds. If you're more comfortable with the risk of stocks, you could have less, though I would suggest always keeping at least 5-10% in bonds. As you get closer to retirement, any money you anticipate needing for the next 5-10 years should be in bonds, with longer-term savings kept in stocks. Rules of thumb like this will help you automatically rebalance towards bonds as you age. You can modify the rule for your risk tolerance (go with just your age in bonds if you have less risk tolerance, or even your age plus some percent).

Stocks: There are many ways to create diversified collections of stocks to invest in. One of the simplest is to create geographical baskets: Canadian stocks, US stocks, and international stocks. For your total stock allocation (whatever is left after bonds), it's ok to have a bit of a home-country bias. Even though Canada is just a small part of the world economy, I'd suggest going with a pretty much even split between the three main areas.

---

savings account, don't go and buy the car as soon as the account hits $10,000. Keep that $5,000 (or at least some cushion) for actual emergencies, as per the plan. The car can wait until the savings account hits the full $15,000.

The reason for having a bit of home country bias are taxes and currency: there's no good reason to suspect that – over the long term – one currency or another will do better, but there will be fluctuations in relative value. Because you'll most likely be retiring in Canada, it makes sense to keep a large part of your assets in Canadian dollars (and hence, Canadian companies) to protect against any increases in our dollar, which is what you will use to pay for many of your needs. Also, the government encourages people to invest their money in companies that underlie the economy (and employ Canadians), so investing in Canadian companies is usually a bit more tax-efficient than investing in foreign ones.

However, Canada's economy is fairly small by global standards, so it also makes sense to have a large allocation to the US (our largest trading partner and also one of the largest stock markets) and the other developed nations around the world. Many goods are priced in global markets and the price merely converted to Canadian dollars in the stores for you, so you should likely have some holdings that are exposed to these global markets. Exactly how to split up your asset allocation is up to you, but an even 3-way split between Canada, the US, and the rest of the world is a good starting point – and like much of this book, getting close enough and making it easy is better than spending the time and effort to try to perfect it down to the last percentage point. We'll go into more detail on how to do this in the *Putting It Into Practice* section.

Asset Allocation: Special Situations

Some special situations can come into play for how to create your asset allocation.

One is what you do for a living: many companies offer their employees discounts on the company stock. Those employees then take advantage of the discount and end up with large amounts of that company's stock in their asset allocation. I would say that it's great to take advantage of a company stock purchase plan if you can: it's basically free money if the company matches your investment or gives you a discount. But, you should sell the stock as soon as you're allowed to (it's common to be locked-in for one-to-two years after buying before you can sell) and keep the overall exposure to a reasonable limit (e.g. don't let your holdings in your employer exceed 10% of your total investments). Some companies do well, and the employees who bought stock do well right along with them. But, some companies don't do well, and then people find that not only do they lose their job as the company flounders, but their investments are also worthless (e.g. many Enron and Nortel employees). You put yourself more at risk by having both your job and your investment portfolio tied to one company.

Similarly, anyone who works in the real estate industry (as a tradesperson involved in renovations or construction, a real estate agent, broker, etc.) also should not invest a large part of their net worth in real estate. Despite this sage advice, many realtors find themselves with rental condos, likely due to familiarity. Similarly, people who are knowledgeable about an area tend to over-estimate their expertise and heavily invest in companies involved in that area, even though there is usually a large disconnect between technical knowledge and investing prowess.

And real estate itself is an asset class, though an illiquid one. It's hard to buy in small chunks, and it often involves borrowing large sums of money in the form of a mortgage to purchase. When you're young, if you decide to buy instead of rent it's quite difficult to get real estate to be any sensible proportion of your assets: it's almost certainly going to be nearly 100% at first. I can only suggest that you try to reduce the exposure as much as possible, especially as you get into your 40s and 50s (by then your real estate should be <40% of your total net worth). If you're a renter and you want some real estate exposure, you can buy what are known as Real Estate Investment Trusts (REITs). They're not quite the same as owning a house (they are arguably a *better* investment[36]), but you can buy in small increments via exchange-traded funds (tickers[37] VRE, XRE, or ZRE on the Toronto exchange).

Others may try to persuade you into investing in other asset classes like precious metals (gold, silver, platinum) or other commodities (oil, wheat, sugar, coffee). Though an argument can be made for these, the recommended weightings and expected long-term returns are small enough that, in my opinion, it's not worth the effort.

Another special situation would be the case where you have a defined benefit pension through work. In that case

---

[36] Briefly, REITs are diversified across several properties and cities, with many long-term commercial tenants. They are operated by professions solely as investments – they don't pay any price because they fell in love with a property. And they're liquid.

[37] A ticker symbol is a short code used to identify a particular security (stock or fund) on an exchange. They are usually 3 or 4 letters, sometimes with extensions to signify classes of shares.

you may have enough of a guarantee that your future spending needs will be met that a much larger portion of your savings can be risked in equities than would be the case for someone else with your age and psychology but without the pension assurance.

Rebalancing

The markets won't move up in lock-step: you may find your US stocks are down one year while Canadian stocks and bonds are up. When that happens, it's time to bring your asset allocation back into the planned balance – to **rebalance**. To do this for this case, you need to put more money into the US stocks and less into the Canadian stocks and bonds to get the allocation back to your target. You can do this by selling some of what went up to buy some of what went down, but if you're still in your saving years a better method is to change how you distribute new contributions, to preferentially buy more of what is now under the target weighting.

For example, if your plan is to have 50% bonds and your current balance was $450 bonds, $500 stocks, and you were contributing $400, you wouldn't simply split the contribution equally (according to the plan), but rather buy enough bonds so that the total *after* the contribution was back to 50%. The calculation is to add up the total value after the contribution is made: $450 + $500 before + the $400 new contribution = $1350. Then find out how much of that should be in each category (50% in bonds, so $675 should be in bonds). Finally, find out how much needs to be added to each group to rebalance (in this case, $675 - $450 currently in bonds = $225 that needs to be added to bonds; leaving $175 to add to stocks).

There's a good spreadsheet for handling this from Canadian Capitalist for a portfolio of mutual funds at www.canadiancapitalist.com/sleepy-portfolio-rebalancing-spreadsheet/ and I have made a larger, more flexible one ideal for ETFs available at www.holypotato.net/?p=1242.

For rebalancing, there are several hotly debated schemes on how to determine when to rebalance. One method is to simply rebalance any time you have new money to contribute, using the calculation above (the spreadsheets make it easy). Sometimes new contributions might not be big enough to fully rebalance, or you may not be able to make new contributions, or you may have set up an automated investment plan – and it's more important to keep the simplicity of that going than to constantly change it to rebalance. In that case it's generally wise to strike a balance between not rebalancing all the time (you don't want to rebalance every last 0.1% deviation from plan), but also to not avoid rebalancing entirely. The two main schools of thought are **time-based rebalancing**, where you only rebalance once or twice per year; and **threshold rebalancing**, where you rebalance any time the target weighting of one component is off by more than some percentage (say 5%), and don't bother otherwise. For threshold rebalancing you can set up a warning in your rebalancing spreadsheet to make monitoring it simple. Either one is sufficiently simple yet effective.

Putting It Into Practice

So now you're ready to dive in. Here's the actual step-by-step method for investing on your own. An over-arching plan will guide your asset allocation and account allocation. Then the mechanical steps of setting up an account and purchasing investments will let you implement your plan. For the implementation part I'll present four options in increasing order of effort required, though the lessons can be applied to other investment options out there, particularly the fourth option on ETFs. How to rebalance and maintain this portfolio – with links to spreadsheets that will help with the rebalancing calculation and record-keeping – will follow, along with a sample planning reference sheet to help you stay on track for the years to come.

Step 1: Make a Plan

Start with a plan and collecting the information you'll need.

- How old are you now?

- When do you want to retire (perhaps select a few years to test early, delayed, and planned retirement scenarios), and how long will you live (or how long a contingency will you plan for)?

- How much money do you make?

- What does your household budget look like? What big expenses do you need to save up for in the near- or medium-term (education, cars, houses, etc.)?

- How much money can you save per year without making any changes to your budget? How much money can you save with some belt-tightening?

The younger you are, the more nebulous your plan may be: there are many possibilities and it's hard to plan for them all. For the younger investor, perhaps the most important points are to identify how much you can save, and what you might need to save for in the nearer term so you know what money you shouldn't put in your long-term retirement investments.

Play around with a spreadsheet program and calculator to see what various scenarios are. Here are some helpful rules of thumb and starting assumptions to help with your planning activity.

Investment returns: assume savings accounts/short-term GICs give zero real[38] return (or even negative real return after taxes). Assume[39] a bond fund gives about 1% real return. Assume stocks give about 6% real return in the very long term. Be sure to see what happens if you're wrong (what if stocks only give 3% real return?) and make contingency plans. You don't necessarily want to plan just for the worst-case scenario, as it's no good to live your life trying to save so much for the future that you don't get to enjoy the present, but at the same time you don't want to fiddle away your productive years and be left with nothing in your old age.

Life in retirement: it can be tough to estimate how much you'll need to live on in retirement. One (hopefully) large component of your budget won't be needed any more: savings. You may also be more frugal in other areas, such as not needing to make a daily commute or to buy quite such expensive clothes as when you're working. If you have/will have children, by the time you're in retirement you probably won't need to budget for their needs. So it may be safe to assume you'll need less than your current salary to support yourself. On the other hand, if you're in a profession where you expect to earn much more later in your career, you may then become accustomed to a more lavish lifestyle than you *currently* live, and might need to plan on more spending than your present budget in retirement (though still less than your final working years). Similarly, if you have dreams of

---

[38] Recall that real return is what's left after accounting for inflation. So a zero real return might be a 3% nominal return with 3% inflation.

[39] There is very little agreement on what makes for a reasonable estimate of future returns. These starting points are based on my own synthesis of various estimates and methods: for fixed income, simply compare the current inflation rate to the yield-to-maturity; for equities, the 6% figure is a compromise between a long-term *Stocks for the Long Run* average figure and the current estimate from the Shiller PE10 approach.

travelling the globe in your sunset years you may need to save more for that now. A decent starting point is to assume that you'll simply need as much as you're spending now except for the savings portion (so about 85-90% of your current salary). Also keep in mind that you'll have larger, rarer expenses like purchasing a new car or taking a large trip on top of your regular budget.

You may also not need to fully support yourself on your own investments: you may have a company pension, or payments from programs like CPP and OAS, which allows you to assume a smaller needed nest egg.

Your health may be the biggest unknown, as medical expenses may be quite high in old age – and health-related costs may stretch beyond medicine, including paying someone to do work you may do yourself now, like mowing your lawn or clearing your snow. Health will also impact how long you live: you can start with a conservative assumption that you'll live to 95 or 100 at this point in your planning. It's a difficult balance to create a conservative plan, but not to get overly conservative.

Step 2: Determine Your Risk Tolerance and Asset Allocation

Look at the factors in your life that affect your risk tolerance, including your own personality and ability to sleep at night. This is going to be important for figuring out how much you want to put into riskier investments like stocks vs. how much in bonds, GICs, and savings accounts.

Indeed, a dispassionate look at your own psychology may be the most important part of this: if you don't think you'll be able to sit tight and stick to a plan when the news is calling for *the end of capitalism as we know it*, then start with a more conservative allocation that you *will* be able to stick to. If you're ready to accept the consequences of being more aggressive – including lowering your budget or delaying purchases in the future if things go poorly – then go ahead and set yourself up with more equities than the age-based rules of thumb might suggest.

Do not underestimate the importance of behavioural factors in planning and investing – they are easily the major divisions between success and failure. Part of setting up an easy-to-follow plan is to make your own life easy and stress-free, but equally important is that the easier a plan is to follow, the more likely it is that you *will actually follow it*. Understand your own risk tolerance and pick an asset allocation you will stick to.

Assessing your own opinion towards risk can be fraught with problems, granted. Following the 2008/2009 stock market crash some investors felt "scarred" by the experience – or their parents' experience, in the case of many younger investors – and are shunning stock market exposure, with allocations far below what their situations and ages suggest they *should* have. Stories in the media of market manipulation aren't helping either. Others have only seen the constantly rising, relatively low-volatility markets of these past few years from late-2009 through to late-2017, combined with low bond/GIC yields, and are over-invested in equities. If I were to say that "many at this point are under-allocated to equities" it's quite likely that the second group would hear that message, rather than the first group which needs to.

Look at your plan and what you'll need to hold aside in cash for your short-term and emergency funds. Then, start splitting up the rest of the money. The table below will serve as a guideline for creating your own asset allocation. Remember that you can't know the future returns, so there's little value in trying to nail these down much more precisely than to the nearest 5% or so. The middle "default suggestion" column should be *close enough* to serve as a starting point for just about anyone reading this book, to give you respectable long-term returns with acceptable levels of risk.

While your risk tolerance will be the main thing determining how much to keep in fixed income vs. equities, there isn't a hard-and-fast rule to decide how to split up the equity portion between Canadian, US, and international markets. An even split is *close enough*, easy to stick to, and a good starting point in my opinion. However, Canada is only a tiny portion of the global market, so there's an argument to be made for lower domestic exposure; on the other hand some may be anchored to historical portfolios (and those of their peers) from advisors that have much higher home biases, and currency volatility and tax treatment can be arguments for a larger home bias. There's no right answer. What's more important is to pick something reasonable and stick to it – don't keep adjusting your portfolio's asset allocation every time an article arguing one way or the other surfaces.

Asset Allocation Guide

Component	Minimum Recommended	Default Suggestion	Maximum Recommended
Bonds/fixed income	5% of total	Your Age – 10 (in %)	65% of total*
Canadian Stocks	10% of equities	1/3 of equities	60% of equities
US Stocks	10% of equities	1/3 of equities	50% of equities
International Stocks	10% of equities	1/3 of equities	50% of equities

* pre-retirement – in retirement, or even close to it, you may wish to have more in fixed income.

Step 3: Account Allocation

Now that you know what you want to invest in in terms of cash, bonds, and stocks, and have a long-term plan, you need to decide where to hold your investments: non-registered, TFSA, RRSP, or most likely, a combination of those. Remember the fruit analogy: these accounts are like the baskets that hold the investment fruits.

I mentioned in the section on the different account types that I like to recommend using the TFSA first, if only because it's easier to get money out of a TFSA if needed. Whichever order makes the most sense for you, fill your registered accounts (TFSA, RRSP, RESP) first to make the most of your tax shelter room and minimize the burden of reporting and paying taxes.

It is best to keep the short-term savings and emergency funds either in a non-registered account or a TFSA, because it is more difficult to withdraw from an RRSP[40].

Then there's the question of what goes where. It is possible to split it up so that each account becomes like a miniature of the overall asset allocation plan: 10% in bonds, 30% in each of the stock indexes in each of the TFSA, RRSP, and non-registered accounts for example. **This is a very good default position**: trying to optimize by selectively putting some assets in specific baskets can make it a lot more complicated to follow and rebalance your portfolio, and most of the benefits of getting more

---

[40] To be precise, it's not difficult so much as it is just undesirable: you lose your contribution room, and have to pay income tax on the amount withdrawn. Tax sheltering with the option to withdraw if needed is what the TFSA is ideal for.

complicated are only available when using ETFs (more on that in *Burrowing Deep* later). There can be some advantages to making things more complex – but as always, balance complexity with your ability to stick to a plan.

In general, interest income is the most highly taxed, so the *traditional* rule-of-thumb is that bonds should be the first to be sheltered in a TFSA or RRSP – which one doesn't matter from a tax perspective, though I might again recommend putting bonds in the TFSA first. That's because if disaster does strike it's easier to withdraw from the TFSA, and it will likely be the bonds you'll want to sell.

Stocks are taxed more favourably, but still taxed. Only half of your realized[41] capital gains count towards your income for the year, and a complicated tax credit system for dividends makes that component of equity returns relatively tax-efficient as well. Canadian stocks are taxed least of all, so the *traditional* rule-of-thumb is that perhaps they should be the last to be placed in a tax shelter if space is limited – but again, there isn't much difference as to whether the TFSA or RRSP would be best.

US stocks are a bit peculiar because there *is* a best tax shelter for those: the RRSP. This has to do with a small bit of international tax law: the US IRS taxes dividends from US companies going to Canadian investors, but has a tax treaty with Canada to recognize the RRSP as a tax shelter so they don't apply this withholding tax to dividends going to stocks held in a Canadian RRSP. The tax treaty doesn't cover TFSAs, so it's best to put your US equities in the RRSP. However, this exemption within an

---

[41] You "realize" a capital gain when you sell the fund, or move it from a non-registered account into a registered one (TFSA, RRSP, etc.). Just having the value increase does not make a capital gain taxable.

RRSP *only* applies if you hold US funds directly: a Canadian-based fund or ETF that holds US equities on your behalf will also have the withholding tax applied on your behalf, even in an RRSP. The effect is not huge: with a current yield of about 2% on US indexes, and a 15% withholding tax, it's like adding 0.3% to the fund's MER. If you wish to buy a US ETF directly to avoid that you'll have to convert your Canadian dollars to US dollars – more on that process later – which adds costs that may offset your savings. In the end, it may not be worth worrying about.

Challenging the traditional rule-of-thumb of prioritizing bonds in your tax shelter space is the current interest rate environment. Though interest income from bonds, savings accounts, and GICs is taxed at your full marginal rate, with low interest rates the total tax you have to pay is not very high. If you had $10,000 more to invest than you could shelter in your TFSA and RRSP, and if your marginal tax rate was 33%, then making 3% in a bond fund or GIC would lead to a tax bill of $99. If you instead decided to leave the equity portion of your portfolio outside your tax-sheltered registered accounts and had a 9% capital gain, that would be taxed at *half* the effective rate but still lead to a *larger* tax bill of $148.50. Deciding which component to shelter then depends not just on the tax efficiency but the relative performance and total tax. Unfortunately, we can't know that in advance.

Ultimately this is perhaps not worth worrying about trying to optimize: instead focus on what makes sense for your situation and ability to stick to the plan – and the monitoring burden. If you run into a financial emergency then you will likely look to tap your fixed income holdings first to get you through. If those are already non-registered then you will be able to access them more quickly and easily. However, if you are afraid you might be tempted to spend your savings frivolously if they are easily accessible, then perhaps having a more esoteric Canadian equity fund as your non-registered holding would help you stick to your plan.

And of course, when it's not possible to know what will end up being optimal in advance, it may be best to just diversify and keep it simple, which may mean replicating your portfolio in each account.

A twist is that if you are keeping fixed income in a non-registered account, then it might make sense to look to a GIC or savings account over a bond fund, simply for reasons of tracking and paperwork. Bonds can fluctuate in value as interest rates change – this is part of what makes them good complements to equities in times of turmoil, as bonds may increase in value while stocks decrease if interest rates are decreasing at the same time. That means though that in addition to interest income you'll have to track your cost base and report any capital gains or losses[42]. With a GIC or savings account you get *some* of the same safety features of a bond, but will get a very simple tax slip at reporting time just for the interest income you have to declare.

Finally, if you do have investments in your non-registered account and more tax-sheltered contribution room opens up in future years, you don't have to sell your non-registered investments just to buy them again inside your TFSA or RRSP: you can make what's known as an

---

[42] Note that it is especially advantageous to look at GICs/savings accounts over bonds when bonds are at a "premium." This happens when interest rates have fallen within the duration of the bond: as rates fall, the price of the bond goes up so the total return equals the new interest rate. However for tax purposes you pay full bore on the interest income, while the deduction for the capital loss is only worth half as much. If you can get a GIC for nearly the same posted yield-to-maturity, then that should be the way to go in non-registered accounts.

"in-kind" contribution. It will require placing a call to your brokerage to make it happen[43]. For tax purposes, making an in-kind contribution counts as though you had sold and repurchased – known as a "deemed disposition" – and you must pay tax on any capital gains. Note though that you will not be allowed to claim any capital losses, so in that case it may work to your advantage to sell, claim the loss, and contribute the cash to buy something else in your TFSA/RRSP.

When deciding your account allocation and you want to optimize across accounts, remember to always fill registered accounts first. Whether the TFSA or RRSP will be optimal for you depends on your circumstances, but in general start by maximizing your TFSA room. If you're using ETFs, you may want to preferentially put your US equity component in your RRSP to be as tax efficient as possible, though the small savings may not be worth the hassle – see *A Twist: US ETFs* on page 152 for what's involved (and there's no benefit to attempting that with TD e-series funds). If you have more to invest than you have contribution room, then something will end up in a non-registered account, which should preferentially be your fixed income or Canadian equities – which one will depend on what makes sense to you based on estimated future returns and what will best help you stick to your plan and respond to emergencies.

---

[43] As of 2018, TD Direct Investing customers can use the web platform to make in-kind contributions themselves.

Step 4: Create an Account and Invest!

With your plan of attack all prepared, the next step is to actually set up an account and invest. Below I will detail four excellent options using low-cost index mutual funds or exchange-traded funds (ETFs) at Tangerine, a robo-advisor service, TD Direct Investing, and Questrade. Each one provides greater cost savings at the trade-off of increased complexity.

In my opinion, TD Direct Investing[44] and their e-series index mutual funds represents the best balance between cost savings and effort required. This is not because I receive any kind of compensation from TD, but rather because I truly believe that the e-series index funds are the hands-down winner for investors starting out. They offer the ability to invest in passive stock and bond indexes, in non-registered, TFSA, RESP, and RRSP accounts, with low MERs on the funds and (if you satisfy certain conditions) no other annual fees. Then when your account grows larger and you want to move to ETFs, TD Direct Investing will not be *much* more expensive than Questrade and you'll already be familiar with the platform; if you don't want the added complexity, the fees are reasonable enough to use them forever.

Tangerine is a good option for people with smaller accounts. Things are even easier than TD with their investment funds: all you have to do is pick from one of four basic asset allocations, and they will take care of the rebalancing. Just make your regular contributions to the fund you've chosen, which you can easily automate with a preauthorized payment plan. There are no extraneous fees

---

[44] Formerly TD Waterhouse.

beyond the MER. Tangerine is, simply put, as easy as investing gets without paying a commission to have a salesperson do it for you. The simplicity is great, but the MER of the Tangerine funds is more than double that of the TD e-series funds (yet still half that of typical funds). As your assets grow, this cost difference will become more noticeable.

For the absolute cheapest option, commission-free ETFs at Questrade can't be beat. You pay nearly nothing[45] to buy, and a small commission to sell (about $5-10 per trade). And the on-going MER of the ETFs is as low as you can possibly get for investments. However, the order-entry process is a fair bit more complex than with the mutual funds for Tangerine and TD, and you have to deal with rounding off to whole units rather than just investing a given dollar amount.

---

[45] No standard commission to buy. "ECN" fees may apply, which are difficult to explain succinctly. At $0.0035/share, they're roughly a 0.02% one-time fee – not a major factor.

Four Investing Options – Effort vs. Cost

	Tangerine	Robo-advisor	TD e-series	ETFs (Questrade)
Effort required (increasing left to right)	Can invest to the last penny Automatic rebalancing Orders very straightforward Preauthorized purchases	Automatic rebalancing Orders very straightforward Preauthorized purchases	Can invest to the last penny Must rebalance manually Orders very straightforward Preauthorized purchases	Must invest in whole ETF units Must rebalance manually Orders more complex Margin accounts
Typical MER[46]	1.07%	Complex fees (~0.4-1.0%)	0.422%	0.178%
Annual cost for $20,000	$214	$92	$84	$46
Annual cost for $100,000	$1,070	$570	$422	$188
Annual cost for $300,000	$3,210	$1,450	$1,270	$542

There are many other options available: every major bank has an associated discount brokerage arm where you can buy the same ETFs available at Questrade or TD Direct Investing; some banks and mutual fund companies offer relatively low-cost funds that are competitive with Tangerine's. These four options, however, are the archetypical combinations of low fees and convenience at various points along the trade-off. I will provide step-by-steps for using each, along with general information for buying ETFs at brokerages other than Questrade.

---

[46] Assuming 25% in each of a bond fund, Canadian, US, and International equities. For dollar comparisons, assumes $10 in commissions per year. If you decide to shift to ETFs and want to stay with TD Direct Investing, assume that you will have about $40-120/yr in additional commissions over Questrade. Rounded to 3 significant figures. For robo-advisors, the lowest cost option at each level chosen (ModernAdvsior, Nest Wealth).

Step 4a: Investing with Tangerine

Tangerine's all-in-one funds are the laggard in terms of MER costs (1.07%) for the four options here – and even fall behind RBC's[47] 0.7% – but they make the process as simple as possible by having all four indexes included in a single fund, which are automatically rebalanced. The simplicity may make the extra fees worthwhile for some, particularly smaller accounts. And they're still half the cost of the actively managed mutual funds Canadians typically buy. Tangerine can be a great choice when you're starting out and you don't have much to invest: you can get started very quickly, and get a no-fee chequing and/or savings account at the same time.

All you have to do is choose how much of your asset allocation should be in bonds, and buy the corresponding fund. Here are the details on the four options, including the fund codes (which you can use to look up information in financial databases, but aren't needed within Tangerine itself to buy or sell).

- 0% bonds – Tangerine Equity Growth Portfolio; INI240

- 25% bonds – Tangerine Balanced Growth Portfolio; INI230

- 40% bonds – Tangerine Balanced Portfolio; INI220

- 70% bonds – Tangerine Balanced Income Portfolio; INI210.

---

[47] Which doesn't get a mention because four separate funds are just as much work as TD's e-series but not as cheap. If you're already with RBC then maybe you can consider them as an alternative.

For each fund, the non-bond portion is split equally between Canadian, US (S&P 500) and international (MSCI EAFE) equity components.

Tangerine exemplifies the concept of keeping it simple yet effective – which is what this book is about – but the ~0.65% difference in cost between Tangerine and the TD e-series funds does add up, and robo-advisors have emerged as a competitive alternative for a relatively hands-off option. However, the simplicity and track-record may appeal to you. Particularly for small non-registered accounts, Tangerine's simplicity may be worth the cost: the fact that your entire allocation is within a single mutual fund means that if you have a taxable account, rebalancing does not mean "realizing" any capital gains, further simplifying the burden of tracking and reporting. For investors able to shelter all their funds in their RRSP and TFSA, robo-advisors may be a better choice.

To create an account visit https://www.tangerine.ca/app/#/enroll and choose "investing" for the "Choose Accounts" step.

As you go through the set-up process Tangerine will ask you some questions to identify your risk tolerance, and based on this will automatically pick the right fund for you. If you disagree with the system's choice, you can amend your answers to fine-tune the selection, and further in the process they will even give you the scoring key. Within a given account you can only hold one of the funds, however you can designate your non-registered, TFSA, and RRSP to hold different funds if they have different purposes by changing your responses to the risk profile questionnaire as each is opened. To change your risk tolerance (and hence fund selection) later, you will have to call them, it can't be done online.

After the questionnaires and other data is entered just print, sign, and mail or fax your paperwork in to create your account. Note that if you are also opening a chequing or savings account at Tangerine that you should do that first[48].

You'll have to mail in a cheque to fund the account initially if you don't already have a chequing or savings account with Tangerine. This will also link your chequing account to the mutual fund account, making the process of setting up an automatic contribution later simple. From within the account set up process, you can create your automatic savings program for weekly, bi-weekly, or monthly purchases; or, do it later through your account on Tangerine's website.

When you want to make additional purchases or sales, click on your investing account when logged in to Tangerine, then click on "Buy". You will only have the one fund option per account (non-registered, TFSA, RRSP) – notice in the screenshot how the description of the account is not a drop-down.

---

[48] If you wish to help support me, you can enter my Orange Key (a referral code) in the application: it will give you a $50 bonus on your chequing or savings account (but unfortunately not a mutual fund account alone). My key is: 41498982S1

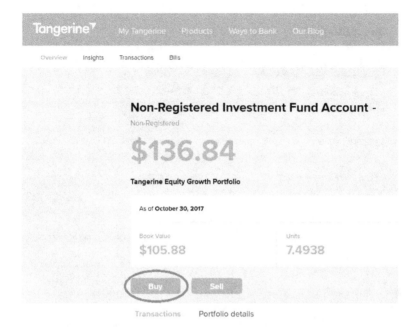

You will then walk through the process of purchasing funds. First, you'll choose which account to pull the money from (e.g. your Tangerine chequing account, or an account linked from another bank). Then you'll have the choice of making a single purchase, or setting up an automatic ongoing program.

For an ongoing purchase plan, the next screen will let you choose how often you'll make the automatic contributions (weekly/biweekly/monthly), and whether it should run indefinitely or just for a certain period.

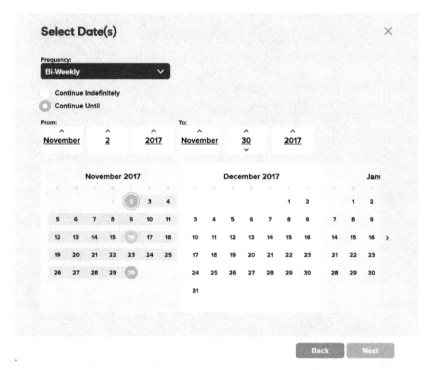

Then you simply choose the amount to invest for your one-time or recurring purchase, and confirm whether you're using borrowed money to make the investment. You'll have one more review before confirming, and a note about how many days it will take for the trade to settle. After submitting your order, you'll get a summary and a confirmation number (which you'll only need if something goes wrong and you have to call in).

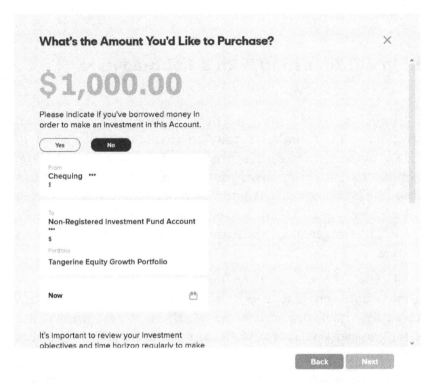

As you can see, Tangerine has designed their entire process to be very simple and user-friendly, including the interface. You make your asset allocation decision just once when you set up your account, and then they will ensure that you automatically follow it without fail as you continue to invest. The ability to set up automatic contributions is put right in front of your eyes every time you make a purchase or sale, encouraging you to make your savings and investing automatic and regular – which is a good way to make sticking to your plan easy on yourself.

While they are the most expensive option by a decent margin, that higher MER does bring some value in simplicity – and it's still much cheaper than most Canadian mutual funds. Particularly for smaller portfolios, they can be a great low-effort choice.

Step 4b: Investing with a Robo-advisor

Robo-advisors are a new option for Canadian investors. They make it easy to invest in a portfolio of ETFs by automating the process of buying and selling: similar to Tangerine, you just put money in the account and they will get it invested and keep it to your target allocation. The all-in cost typically falls somewhere between Tangerine's fund and a portfolio of TD e-series funds.

Unlike the other three methods, there isn't an easy choice between just one or two companies to feature an in-depth how-to, and even if there was, things are changing so fast it would be out-of-date by the time this book hit the shelves.

Indeed, when the first edition of *The Value of Simple* was sent to the printer in 2014, robo-advisors didn't exist in Canada; three launched that year, and there are nine as of mid-2017; in a short span of time we've seen one takeover, and many rounds of interface changes, fee changes, and shifts in the portfolios used.

Many are quick to point out that "robo-advisor" is a bit of a misnomer, as in (almost) all cases, *people* are involved in choosing the portfolio – the automation is limited to buying the ETFs in the prescribed allocation, and rebalancing to maintain that allocation – and there isn't a whole lot of advising happening. Nonetheless, the name has stuck, and is much catchier than "online automated investment manager."

Deciding which robo-advisor is best for you is a bit of a challenge: starting with the most basic part of a comparison – the fees charged – is difficult in its own right. Each firm advertises a fee that has multiple tiers: usually based on a percentage of what you invest with them, though Nest Wealth charges a flat monthly fee (which can work out well for large accounts). As if that weren't complicated enough, the MERs of each ETF in the portfolio are important to the overall cost, but are not included in the large-print advertised fee, and can be hard to find even in the fine print. And with some firms' model portfolios using fairly costly choices, the cost of the underlying funds can sometimes rival the service's headline fee. Some firms also pass along charges from their custodian brokers, like trading fees or account administration fees, adding to the nightmare of comparison shopping.

To help figure it all out on an even playing field, Sandi Martin (http://springplans.ca) and I created a comparison tool at https://autoinvest.ca (now owned & managed by Kyle Prevost[49] & Justin Bouchard).

Beyond the fees charged, each robo-advisor has its own philosophy for building portfolios, as well as various other services (from on-demand advice for some simple financial planning questions to optimizing your holdings across your RRSP/TFSA/non-registered accounts). Bear those factors in mind as you compare your options.

The main advantage of robo-advisors is that they make it easy to invest at a reasonable cost, providing automatic investing and rebalancing in fairly sensible portfolios. The portfolios will not necessarily be as simple as those proposed here – with automation for your purchases and rebalancing, there isn't as much of a downside to complexity. The firms seem to relish in slicing-and-dicing with their model portfolios, perhaps to add an air of

---

[49] You may also want to read Kyle's guide to robo-advisors at: https://youngandthrifty.ca/complete-guide-to-canadas-robo-advisors/

sophistication or to reinforce the perception that investing is complicated. Many firms do stray from a purely passive philosophy, but there are no points for purity in the world, and as long as the portfolios are broadly diversified and the fees are reasonable, I'm not too concerned with that given the convenience they can offer.

However, those complex portfolios present one of the downsides to using the services: if you have a non-registered account, you are in for *a lot* of tracking for tax purposes. A portfolio with 10 positions and automatic bi-weekly purchases will leave you with ~260 transactions to track at the end of the year for tax purposes (vs. say 16 if you're making manual purchases for a 4-fund portfolio every quarter, or 48 for monthly purchases). And automatic rebalancing can lead to more realized gains to report than a once-a-year manual check-in. Given that the tracking can be about as much work as just making the purchases yourself, the value proposition isn't quite as strong for investors with non-registered portfolios[50].

Robo-advisors, by automating much of the day-to-day investment process *should* help control bad investor behaviour and make it easy to stick to a plan for long-term success. They are experimenting in this area to try to do even better: during a market dip early in their history, several sent out reassuring emails to their clients reminding them that this is all part of investing and to stick to the plan; of course, some clients had no idea there was a correction happening at all, so the email may have backfired. Some are now testing segmented auto-reassurance systems, and we'll see how those work out for keeping clients on track.

---

[50] Some robo-advisors may track the adjusted cost bases (ACB) and help prepare reports for tax filing – or may do so in the future – but I've looked and can't find clear confirmation that they will, so I'd assume the work will fall to the investor.

However, a major issue that I see is in the smartphone apps. One firm has said that a third of their users check in on their smartphone app *daily*. **There is absolutely no good that can come from checking in on a passive investment portfolio daily.** It feels good to see the gains in a rising market – and it's great for the firm, who have high "engagement" numbers and a greater chance of finding new clients through word-of-mouth. But as soon as those investments start going down, the person checking every day is going to feel more pain, worry, and distress than someone who only checks in every quarter or every year. If you go with a robo-advisor, I urge you to avoid using the app as much as possible: let yourself reap the benefits of automation.

A minor issue is the flux in the industry, which is to be expected for such a young, rapidly growing industry. We're still in the early adopter phase for robo-advisors, so users should expect that the user interfaces, services, and portfolios will be tweaked, as might the pricing model – the competitive pressure so far has mostly led to lower costs and portfolio changes that use less expensive products, but that trend could reverse at any time. We've seen some growing pains in terms of customer service, which may crop up from time to time (but even the big banks can find their help desks overloaded at certain times like near the RRSP deadline or the first week of January).

In short, robo-advisors are fantastic options for people who want to get investing with a minimum of work and are willing to pay a bit more than the next two options, particularly those who will invest solely within their TFSA and RRSP. Just bear in mind that you will need to understand your risk tolerance, that the headline fees will not cover the total cost, and you may have some work cut out for you on the tracking and reporting side if you have a non-registered (taxable) account.

Step 4c: Investing with TD Direct Investing

TD Direct Investing is my personal top choice and what I recommend most often. The phone staff have been in my experience excellent, and there are no fees for buying/selling the e-series mutual funds[51], which themselves have the lowest MER in Canada (except for ETFs). It is also a highly rated stock brokerage, so you'll be set up to move to ETFs if/when your account grows to the point where it's warranted and you have the desire. As of March 2016, TD charges $100 per year (in $25 amounts every 3 months) for accounts smaller than $15,000. You can avoid this fee by setting up a systematic investment plan of at least $100/mo, which works great with automating your e-series purchases. There's no minimum amount needed to open an account, though because of the fees you should only choose them if you have $15,000 to invest *or* will be able to contribute regularly with the automatic contributions.

More importantly, the TD e-series mutual funds strike a great balance between complexity and costs.

I will quickly note that you can also buy TD e-series mutual funds through TD's Mutual Fund (TDMF)[52] arm. You can set up an account in person at a bank branch or online, and then convert your mutual funds account to one capable of holding e-series (the form is available at

---

[51] Note that the e-series funds have such low fees because everything is self-service: the staff in the branch **cannot** help you with e-series funds.

[52] TD is made up of essentially separate companies loosely working together: TDMF operates and is regulated differently than TD Direct Investing/Waterhouse, but both allow you to buy TD e-series funds.

www.tdcanadatrust.com/document/PDF/mutualfunds/t
deseriesfunds/tdct-mutualfunds-tdeseriesfunds-
convertaccount.pdf). A TDMF account is *supposed* to be
simpler and for the less-savvy investor, with no fees and
access only to mutual funds (no stocks or ETFs), and you
can even place orders in person with branch salespeople
(for their *other* mutual funds). Unfortunately, the branch
and phone staff at TDMF *cannot* help you with the low-
cost e-series mutual funds. And there is no ability to hold
cash in a TDMF account, so purchases and contributions
are conflated into one step, which I personally find more
confusing than the brokerage model, and makes
preparing for a withdrawal complicated. There have also
been cases where people have accidentally withdrawn
from their RRSPs when trying to sell their funds because
selling is tied to withdrawing[53]. Finally, the know-your-
client forms can restrict your ability to invest using an
asset allocation that you think is appropriate unless you
answer all of the questions in the most aggressive way
possible.

A brokerage account – like a TD Direct Investing or
Questrade account (which I will further detail below) – is
completely self-directed, whereas a mutual fund account
may involve meeting with a salesperson to periodically
review your paperwork, which subjects you to their sales
pitches that might draw you away from the efficient e-
series funds towards ones with higher MERs. Even if they
offer to help you to buy "index funds", assisted
transactions will likely end up purchasing the more
expensive "i-series" funds rather than the e-series you
intended. Finally, if you do want to move to ETFs as your

---

[53] If you do go with TDMF and want to get out of a TD e-series
fund but not withdraw from your account, instead of "selling"
look to "switch" to a money market fund. Same for rebalancing,
use the "switch" function rather than selling one to buy
another.

assets grow into the six-digits you will need to open a new account at a brokerage anyway. The supposedly simpler TDMF account leads to trouble more often than not, hence my recommendation to go with the TD Direct Investing route.

To set up your account with TD Direct Investing, visit www.tdwaterhouse.ca/apply/index.jsp and follow the instructions. In the process you can select non-registered, TFSA, RRSP, or all three, whatever applies to your situation. I would recommend always including a non-registered account even if you don't think you need it. Select **cash account**[54]. Do not select option or short selling trading features. Those are again features that are not for the readers of this book; if you change your mind on margin, options, or short-selling, you can modify your account with the phone representatives after it's open.

You will have to provide some personal information to open the account, and may be required to provide a signature and a copy of your photo ID to a branch or directly to TD Direct Investing by mail/fax.

After a few weeks (sooner if you're lucky) your account will be set up and activated, you'll get a welcome package, and importantly, a login for WebBroker. You'll need to transfer money into your account before you can buy any mutual funds. From other banks, this can be set up as an electronic bill payment (just like paying any other bill, except you pay yourself!), and from a TD Canada Trust chequing account the transfer is even easier: just click on transfers when you're logged into EasyWeb. When transferring money in from a chequing account always use your non-registered account so you don't accidentally over-contribute to your RRSP or TFSA. You can easily

---

[54] Margin accounts allow you to borrow against the value of your investments to buy more stocks/ETFs. This adds significant risk and is only for advanced investors.

transfer between sub-accounts within the WebBroker system once the money is in.

To buy e-series funds you'll need to know the fund code. To find the fund code (and more details on the funds), visit tdcanadatrust.com/mutualfunds/prices.jsp and select e-series. Here are the four you're most likely to need.

Table of TD E-series Funds

Fund Name	Fund Code	MER	Index Tracked
TD Canadian Bond Index (e-series)	**TDB909**	0.50%	DEX Universe Bond
TD Canadian Index (e-series)	**TDB900**	0.33%	TSX Composite Index (Canadian equities)
TD US Index (e-series)	**TDB902**	0.35%	S&P 500 Index (US equities)
TD International Index (e-series)	**TDB911**	0.51%	MSCI EAFE Index (international equities)

For all four funds there is a minimum $100 purchase. Note though that you don't have to buy in $100 increments: once you meet the $100 minimum, you can buy in any amount. So if you have $450 to invest, you could invest $100 in the bond index and $116.66 in each of the others if you so choose. You can also sign up for a preauthorized purchase plan (PPP), where a certain amount can be automatically taken from your chequing account and invested for you monthly. For that plan the minimum monthly contribution is just $25 per fund. These can be set up by phone for TDDI (or through the EasyWeb interface for TDMF accounts).

Once you have your account open, with money in it, and have planned out your asset allocation so that you know what to buy, it's time to dive in and make your first purchase!

First, click on Buy/Sell on the top of the screen:

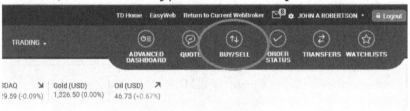

Then, click on the "mutual funds" tab.

Select the account to buy in (Cash, TFSA, RRSP, etc) at the top, and with "action" whether you want to **buy**, sell, or switch. Then, enter the fund code and select the full fund name that pops up – this will display some details about the fund, and allow you to see the name that goes with the fund code to make sure you didn't make a typo.

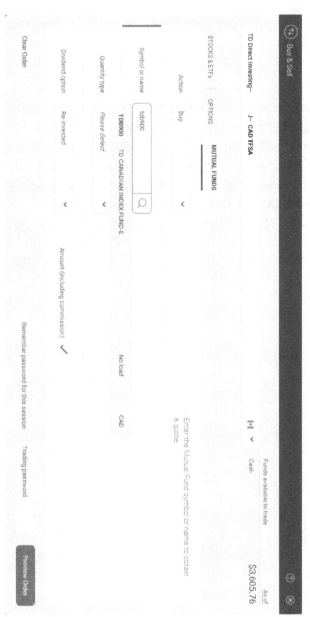

Here I've entered the code for the Canadian Index (TDB900), and indeed, that is the name that comes up, along with the –e at the end to indicate that it is a low-cost e-series fund (there are several funds called "TD Canadian Index Fund" each of a different "series" with a different set of fees/MER – you want the low-cost e-series version).

You can place your order by entering the total amount in dollars, or choosing the number of units you want with "quantity type". For example, on the day I took this screenshot the Canadian Index was at $23.90 per unit, so if I chose 10 units that would end up costing *about* $239.00 – I say about because the price is usually the last day's price, and not actually the price you would buy your mutual fund units at – the trade won't settle until the end of the day (or the next day if you enter your trade after 3pm). The easier and much more common method is to just enter the amount you want to buy in terms of dollar amount.

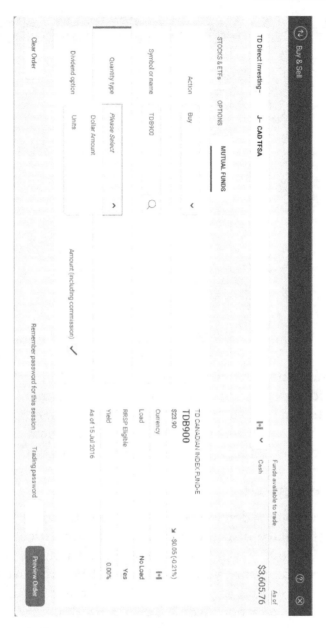

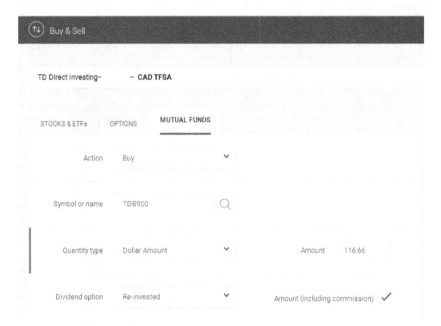

The final options – "dividend option" and "amount" can be left alone. The dividend option refers to whether the dividends that the fund pays out are automatically re-invested for you into new units of the same fund, or deposited as cash into your account. Generally, for automatic long-term investing, you'll want them to be re-invested. The commission one doesn't matter whether you check it or not as there is no commission to buy or sell the e-series funds.

Once your order is set up, press next, where you will get a summary of the order and a chance to confirm or cancel it. You may see some warnings on this summary page, including that your order will not be processed with today's price, and if you place your order after markets close in the afternoon you'll see a note that markets are closed for the day and your order will be processed on the next business day. Those are fairly self-explanatory and perfectly normal. So is a warning that the fund you are buying has a minimum holding period – that's just a reminder that you could face early redemption fees if you sell an e-series fund within 30 days of purchasing it. You may also receive a checkbox consenting to receive your Fund Facts documents electronically (along with a link to download them if you wish to).

Another warning is *"TD Direct Investing receives a trailing commission from the issuing company for as long as you hold this investment. See the related offering documents for more details."* This warning is part of mutual fund disclosure rules, but it's unfortunately not very helpful. What this means is that a part of the MER you pay on the TD e-series funds *may* go to TD Direct Investing/Waterhouse. It does *not* mean that you're paying any more in fees than you expect to – a TD e-series fund will still cost you between 0.33% and 0.51%.

Following your approval of the order it goes into the system, and you will get a reference number to write down. You can now see your order on the "Order Status" page (top menu bar). Note that there's an account drop-down here too, and each account (cash/non-registered, TFSA, RRSP) will have its own set of order statuses. It will take a few days (up to 3 business days) before you see the purchase reflected in your account balances – be careful not to spend your cash twice!

And that is very nearly it. Repeat the purchase process for each fund you wish to purchase, in each account. You can either manually purchase funds as you save up more money to invest, or call TD to set up a preauthorized purchase plan.

While managing four funds and entering the symbols yourself is more work than Tangerine or a robo-advisor, it is still quite simple and relatively easy to manage. The interface through WebBroker is fairly intuitive, though the error messages aren't always. TD's e-series funds are less than half the cost of Tangerine's funds and generally[55] cheaper than the all-in cost of a robo-advisor, and are very reasonably priced even for larger accounts. You can, however, invest with even lower fees by using exchange-traded funds in a discount brokerage account, though that will come with some extra complexity.

In TD, purchasing ETFs works similarly. Click on buy/sell in the top menu bar, select the "stocks & ETFs" tab and enter the ETF ticker symbol – see the table in the next section on ETFs and Questrade for the tickers you should be interested in. You will have to select the ETF from the autocomplete list that comes up, and make note of the exchange the securities trade on with the flag icons beside them (this is slightly different than how Questrade's system works). All of the ETFs in the table trade on the Canadian exchanges except for VTI. Otherwise, the process is the same as what is described next for Questrade.

---

[55] NestWealth's fixed fee (plus the relatively low MERs of the underlying funds) can bring the all-in cost below the cost of a TD e-series portfolio for a large enough account – around $400,000. For very small accounts, the "first $5,000 managed free" offers of several robo-advisors can also make their cost dip below that of TD e-series – though you'll probably plan on exceeding that amount in time!

Step 4d: Investing in ETFs

ETFs offer the lowest MERs available, but require a bit more effort and a few more steps to enter your orders. You can purchase ETFs through any discount brokerage, but by letting you buy the cheapest ETFs with no commission to pay when purchasing, Questrade becomes the hands-down winner in terms of low costs when investing. The ETFs themselves are offered by third parties: Blackrock (iShares) and Vanguard are the leaders in Canada, though several other companies offer low-cost index and specialized ETFs. Because they can be purchased over the public stock exchanges, similar instructions will also apply to TD Direct Investing and other brokerages, with the same products available.

With a minimum of $5,000, Questrade accounts have no on-going fees[56]. In the TD instructions I made a special note to select a cash account – unfortunately Questrade only has margin[57] accounts available. This means you will have to be careful to not borrow money to invest that you don't intend to; though the advantage is you don't need to worry as much about accidentally rounding up and over-

---

[56] The minimum to open an account is $1,000, and the account fees charged between $1,000 and $5,000 can be avoided by making at least one trade every three months.

[57] A margin account is like a cash account combined with a line of credit: you can borrow against the value of your stocks and bonds in the account to invest further. For example, if you had $100,000 of your own money in the account, you might be permitted to borrow an additional $50,000 to buy even more stocks. Borrowing to invest adds significant risk and is only recommended for advanced investors. Though margin accounts are the only option at Questrade, you do not have to borrow anything.

buying ETFs in a non-registered account because you can borrow the difference. The main thing to notice is that "buying power" is how much they will let you borrow and is not the same as the amount of cash you have to invest. Also, even if you have cash in one currency (e.g. CAD), if you buy in another one (e.g. USD) you may end up taking out a loan in that currency rather than converting.

The ETF marketplace is constantly shifting as new funds are released, and MERs change due to competitive pressures. Be sure to check the errata page (valueofsimple.ca/errata) or other up-to-date online sources for your ETF ticker symbols and MERs. The table below has a selection of ETFs that fit particular asset classes, which should help you quickly build a diversified portfolio. You can choose any of the various funds here for each category, or build yours using some of the multitude of ETFs that didn't make the short list. Just be aware that it's easy to fall down a rabbit hole of reading the details on different ETFs and trying to figure out which is *best* for your portfolio. Try to keep in mind that a few basis points of cost difference is not going to make or break your financial plan and that in many cases the differences between ETFs is extremely small and likely not worth the mental energy of anguishing over.

Table of Exchange-Traded Funds

ETF Name	Ticker/ Exchange	Category	Management Fees and Alternatives
Canadian Bond Index	**ZAG** / Toronto	Bond	Fees of 0.09%. Alternatives include VAB (0.12%), XQB (0.12%), XBB (0.09%)
Canadian Capped Composite Index	**XIC** / Toronto	Canadian Equity	Fees of 0.05%. Alternatives include VCN (0.05%), VCE (0.05%), ZCN (0.05%)
US Total Market Index[58]	**VUN** / Toronto	US Equity	Fees of 0.15%. Alternatives include S&P 500 funds XUS (0.10%), ZSP (0.10%) VFV (0.16%)
Developed Excluding North America Index	**XEF** / Toronto	International Equity	Fees of 0.20%. Alternatives include ZEA (0.20%), VIU (0.20%)

The first step is to create an account[59] with Questrade by visiting: http://www.questrade.com/account/online

When you create your account the options are not all displayed in the first view; if you want a non-registered account ("individual margin" at Questrade) as well as a TFSA and RRSP, you'll need to click on the "packaged" tab. Below the choice of account is a section where you

---

[58] Or combine US and International market allocations with one fund such as XAW (management fee of 0.20%) or VXC (0.25%).

[59] If you're opening an account you can use my referral code, embedded in the link below, called a QPass: 356624159378948. This will give you a cash bonus between $25 and $250 depending on how much you deposit, and will also benefit me.

https://start.questrade.com/?oaa_promo=356624159378948

can choose from a variety of selections for "options". At this point you will want to select "none" for all accounts.

You can transfer money in by making a bill payment at your bank. My experience was that it took four days for the transfer to go through and for my account to get activated.

At Questrade there are several *platforms* to choose from, including conventional web-based ones as well as stand-alone applications for your computer, tablet, or smartphone. Some are more advanced and have fees to subscribe to, but the only one you will need is the main web-based platform. From the main Questrade page, click on the "log in" button in the top right or go straight to https://login.questrade.com

For your first log-in, you will also have to agree to the terms and conditions of accessing data for the exchanges that you will use to buy and sell ETFs. These agreements are pretty standard across all brokerages.

Then you will face your Questrade home page, with some high-level information about your account, and many options for collecting your statements, seeing your performance, etc. The main option to look at is the "Trade" option at the top (which you can also reach from the "Accounts" drop-down. Once on your trading page, you'll once again have some high-level information on your account. You can click on "Watchlist" in the left menu, which will by default start pre-populated with some popular stocks.

You can remove those by clicking on the "..." icon in the top-right corner of the pane and choosing "edit this watchlist." I suggest adding the ETFs you will decide to use to your watch list. Just click "add symbol" and start typing the ticker symbol into the box that opens up, and it will provide suggestions. Note that for ETFs that trade on the Toronto exchange you will have to add a .TO suffix to the symbol, though you may see that automatically as you start typing the ticker. American ETFs/stocks generally don't need suffixes.

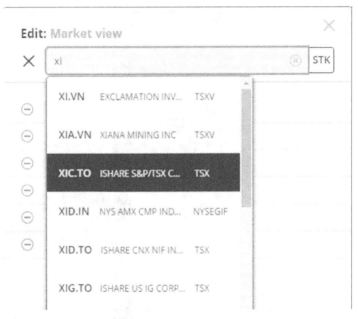

If you start typing the ticker for the ETF or stock you're interested in, you may see it in the auto-complete list after just a few letters. This is one of the few places you will see the spelled-out name of the fund in Questrade.

In the watch list view you can see the current prices for your ETFs of interest. From here you can get right into buying and selling. Click one of the symbols, and you'll be taken to a page with more detailed information and a buttons to buy/sell. Alternatively, you can click on the buy/sell button on the menu bar and then enter the symbol again – but if you start from your watch list and the detailed view page, you will be less prone to making a typo and buying the wrong thing.

After pressing buy or sell, a pop-up will appear where you can enter your order information:

Facing page: In this screenshot, the detailed view for XEF.TO was brought up first, then the order entry popup was launched by clicking the buy/sell button in the top of that page.

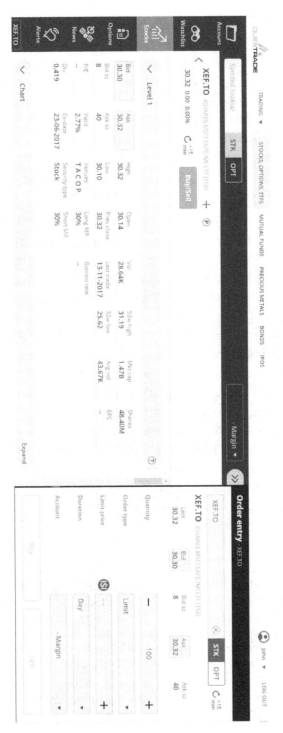

At this point I would like to say that the downside to the low costs of Questrade is that this interface is not the friendliest one for novice investors. However, they have made improvements in recent years[60], including displaying the amount of cash you have available in your account just below the order entry window[61]. That said, the minor inconvenience is offset by the savings on commissions, which can really add up – and if that doesn't work for you, there are instructions for buying ETFs in TD later.

Anyway, in this window you see a fair bit of information. First is some information on the current price of the ETF. The **last price** is displayed underneath the symbol, $30.32 in this screenshot. To the right are the **bid price** ($30.30) and **ask price** ($30.32), which represent the best current orders other people have put in. That is, someone has put in a *bid* to buy shares at $30.30, and someone else is *asking* $30.32 to sell their shares. The difference between these two values is known as the *spread,* and for liquid ETFs it will typically be just a few pennies. So if you want to buy shares, you will have to either pay the ask price and buy right away, or enter your own bid and hope someone else comes along willing to sell for less than the current ask. By far the best, least stressful approach is to just pay the ask price and get your order filled instantly, especially if it is just a few cents per share difference.

---

[60] The downside to those improvements is that they tweak it much more often than other firms, making it hard to learn the quirks for investors who may only check in a few times per year, and annoying authors of how-to books who try to keep their errata sections up-to-date (by the way, don't forget to check the errata occasionally at valueofsimple.ca/errata).

[61] Though do not confuse "buying power" for your cash available – buying power includes the loan they are willing to give you as part of your margin account.

Associated with those bids and asks are the number of shares available for purchase or sale at those prices, known as the bid size (*bid sz* and *ask sz* in the screenshot). The size is in terms of "board lots" (100 shares), so an ask size of 40 means that 4,000 shares are available at the price of $30.32. On the stock market shares can be traded individually, but are typically grouped together into packages of 100, known as a "board lot." For very popular securities (the technical term is *liquid*) there will be enough people selling "odd lots" (amounts other than 100-unit board lots) that you don't have to try to round your order off to 100-share increments. All of the recommended ETFs should have enough liquidity that you can buy or sell in odd lots and not have significant problems getting your order filled. If you dabble in more esoteric names though, this may not be the case. And from time-to-time, even liquid names can experience troubles filling odd lots, which is why using limit orders is important to protect yourself.

If for some reason your order is large, or the ask is "thin" you may be looking to buy or sell more shares than are available in the current ask. In that case, there is a whole line-up of buyers and sellers behind the best prices. For example, someone may be offering 8,000 shares at $30.32 each, and someone else 2,000 shares at $30.35 each, and another 1,000 shares at $30.50. If you were looking to buy 10,500 shares all at once you would exhaust all of those offered at $30.32, buy another 2,000 at $30.35, and then another 500 at $30.50. In practice this scenario is rare for ETFs and you will find that your order gets filled within a few cents of the current ask – but a **limit order** is cheap protection from that rare time when this isn't the case.

To the right of the price information in this screenshot is a small clock icon, indicating that the quotes are delayed by 15 minutes. If I click the refresh button, I'll get an up-to-the-second quote.

After the information about the recent trading are boxes where you can enter your order information. The first is the **quantity**: this represents how many shares you wish to buy. Figuring out how many shares you want is one additional step you must make when looking at ETFs over mutual funds (where you simply enter the dollar value, down to the penny, that you wish to invest). The math is straightforward: take how much you have, subtract an appropriate margin of safety so you don't try to buy more than you have funds available (and to account for trading costs[62]), divide by the price per share you will use as your limit, and round down. Note that this quantity is in actual shares, not board lots, so in the screenshot I am looking to buy 100 individual units of XEF. You can type directly into the box or use the plus and minus buttons to adjust your order size – options within your account preferences will let you set how many shares your quantity moves by for each press of those buttons (default of 10 shares per press).

Under order type you can see several options. Ignore most of them, you will *always* want to select a **limit order**. What a limit order does is enter a maximum price for what you are willing to pay for your shares (or a minimum price you will sell at). Your brokerage will get you the best available price when your order fills, but a limit order protects you against over-paying in the rare case that the market becomes illiquid. In the earlier example of moving up through the *ask* offers, a limit order would set a ceiling to how much you paid to fill your demand. For instance, if you set a limit of $30.35 then

---

[62] At Questrade, you only have to pay tiny ECN fees to buy ETFs, but at other brokerages you may have to pay a commission.

you would buy the shares on offer at $30.32, then those at $30.35, and then stop, leaving part of the order unfilled until either more people came willing to sell at your price (which then became the best *bid*) or the order expired. You would not pay up to the $30.50 (or higher!) level.

Continuing with the options in the screenshot, the account drop-down should be fairly self-explanatory: whether you will be buying in your TFSA, RRSP, or non-registered (margin) accounts. The limit price is where you enter the maximum price you will pay. Next, duration lets you select how long you wish your order to be good for. Day is the default, which means the brokerage will look for shares (or buyers for your shares) to fill your limit order up until the stock market closes for the day. If any part of your order is unfilled, it will be discarded. For buying liquid ETFs where you are looking to buy the market without over-thinking it (so you don't have a particular price point you will wait for), a day order is all you will need. A GTD, or good-til-date, order lets you enter a date in the future; your order will be valid for each day up until your cut-off. GTC stands for good-til-cancelled. The other options are not something you will ever need (indeed, many brokerages don't offer the GTEM/IOC/FOK options that Questrade does, and they get along fine). Finally, you have the buttons for buy and sell.

The Toronto and major American markets are open 9:30am – 4:00pm most weekdays (with exceptions for national and provincial holidays). Ideally, you will enter your orders while the markets are open so that you can see that your orders will fill (usually within a minute) and know what price you will get more accurately, which affects how many shares you can get for a given amount of money. Life is not always ideal, and many people only have time on the evenings or weekends to set up their investments. In that case, you must bear in mind that the last, bid, and ask prices will be out of date for your ETFs.

When the market opens the next business day, the price you may pay will be different. *Usually* there is less than a 1% difference, but there will be a few volatile days which will see larger changes. If you want to ensure your purchase goes through when entering an order after-hours, you may want to add a buffer of about 1% to your limit price.

Now to put it together: to have your buy order fill quickly the *ask* price is what you will pay (and when selling, the *bid* price). Set a limit order to prevent unpleasant surprises, though you may need to allow for a buffer if putting in your orders after-hours to ensure that you do get your order filled the following day. Once you have your limit price set, you can take a buffer for commissions and fees ($10 will do it), and then find how many shares you can afford to buy at that price.

Let's say I had $3000 to invest in XEF at prices from the earlier example. I would start by giving myself a buffer for potential fees[63], and work my scenario out with $2990. The ask price is $30.32, so $2990/$30.32 = 98.615 shares. I can't buy fractional shares, and rounding *off* (to 99) would mean I would invest more money than I had available, which would be a particular problem in a TFSA or RRSP where I had maxed out my contribution room. So I will round *down* to 98 shares. I will enter an order to buy 98 shares with a limit price of $30.32, and leave all the other fields alone, including a *day* duration.

If I was entering this order after hours, I might increase my limit price (and decrease the number of shares) so that if the market (or more directly, my desired ETF) opened higher in the morning, the order would still

---

[63] There are no commissions at Questrade to buy ETFs, but there may be ECN fees; TD will have flat commissions and no possibility of ECN fees. Questrade will have commissions when you sell. In this example I am being conservative.

fill. For instance, a 1% buffer would put my limit price to $30.62, so I would only look to buy 97 shares of XEF (or in Questrade terminology, XEF.TO).

Commission-free purchases can make it easy to buy small amounts, too. Recently I had an order for just 6 shares, a transaction I made after some dividends had built up in the account and I had just over $160 to reinvest.

Once satisfied, I would hit *buy*. This will bring up a confirmation:

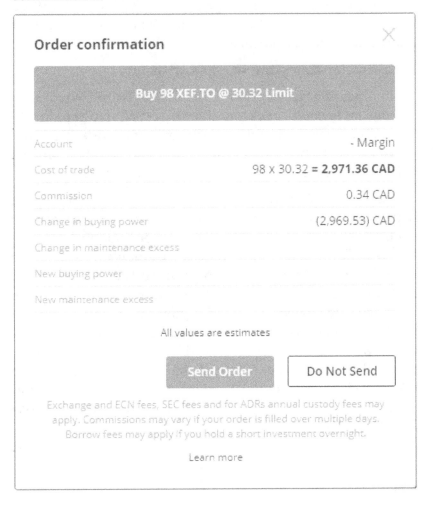

Order confirmation ✕

Buy 98 XEF.TO @ 30.32 Limit

Account	- Margin
Cost of trade	98 x 30.32 = **2,971.36 CAD**
Commission	0.34 CAD
Change in buying power	(2,969.53) CAD
Change in maintenance excess	
New buying power	
New maintenance excess	

All values are estimates

Send Order   Do Not Send

Exchange and ECN fees, SEC fees and for ADRs annual custody fees may apply. Commissions may vary if your order is filled over multiple days. Borrow fees may apply if you hold a short investment overnight.

Learn more

Here I can confirm all the important values before submitting it, including that the total trade value with commission (ECN fees) is below my maximum available cash. I hit *send order*, and a small "O" symbol appears next to XEF in my watch list view, to indicate that I have an open order on that security.

I can follow the same procedure to enter the other orders to build a complete portfolio according to my asset allocation. If this is a non-registered account, I will look for the information on the actual price I paid or received per share, the commissions and fees, and the total number of shares after the order fills, and track that information for tax purposes.

Specifics for Investing in ETFs with TD

If I wanted to buy an ETF in TD WebBroker, after logging in I would click on the "Buy/Sell" button in the top menu, just as if starting with mutual funds (from the previous section). Except now, you would stay on the default "Stocks & ETFs tab" to enter your order.

As before, I have several drop-down selections and boxes to fill in: first to choose the account, second to choose the action (buy or sell), then options for the ETF/security, quantity, price, etc. You don't have to enter them in order. I prefer to skip down to the symbol entry, and then use "get quote" first to confirm that I have the right security selected. For TD you won't enter the .TO suffix, instead you use the drop-down auto-fill that appears as you type to choose the correct ETF. You may notice that the market is designated in the symbol field as CA or US after the ticker symbol (with a space), and typing that in can also work without having to choose from the pop-up).

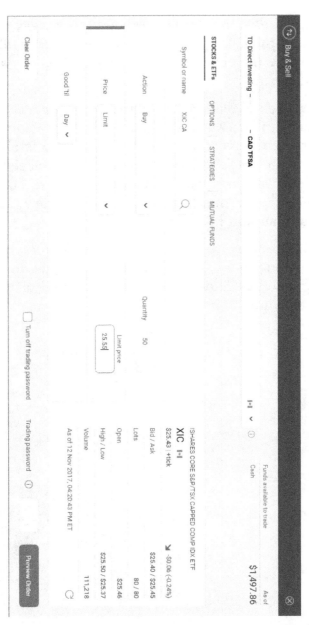

Here I've entered XIC, and we can see in the quote the full name ("iShares S&P/TSX Capped Comp IDX ETF"), which matches up with the name I was expecting to see, related to a TSX index ETF). I've selected a limit order for the "Price" drop-down, and a "Good 'til" of *day*. Because

I've come in after hours, I've decided to increase my limit price above the ask price to make sure the order fills while I'm at work tomorrow and will be unable to watch or adjust the order.

When I click next to enter the order, the TD system stops me with two warnings that I have to check off before I can proceed: a warning that my limit price is above the current ask price, and that the markets are closed for the day. These warnings were of course expected, so I check them off to clear them, hit next again, review the order details and submit my order.

Similar to Questrade, if I had started from my holdings view I could have clicked on "buy" beside one of my existing holdings and saved myself the step of typing in the ticker symbol.

Rebalancing Redux

In the previous section on rebalancing I briefly went over why you want to rebalance, and linked to a spreadsheet that will help you rebalance by buying more or less of each fund to help bring your portfolio back into balance. For most young investors, the regular contributions are large enough relative to the portfolio size that just adjusting new purchases is enough to get the investment portfolio back into line with the plan. However sometimes you may find that more rebalancing is needed than can be achieved with just new purchases. In that case, for e-series with TD you'll find the "switch" option from the order entry handy: it will allow you to sell one fund and buy another in a single step (i.e. switching!). Other than for rebalancing, there isn't much need to worry about the switch option with TD Direct Investing[64]. With ETFs, you will have to enter separate sell and buy transactions – don't forget that there will be commissions to sell for both TD and Questrade, and to buy for TD. Of course, investments with Tangerine funds will automatically rebalance for you.

When it comes time to rebalance it's important to remember what your target allocation was in the first place. After a year or so, you can't trust your memory for that important detail. I highly recommend creating a reference sheet and keeping it somewhere safe that details your plan: your asset allocation, your account and

---

[64] But with TDMF, you can't sell a fund without also withdrawing, so if you need help from a TD rep withdrawing cash (e.g. for the RRSP Home Buyer's Plan), you'll first have to switch your e-series funds to a fund they can help you with, such as the money market fund.

product allocation to meet that, and the details of your savings plan. This will help you better determine when you are off-target, and when corrective action may be needed.

Along with the bare facts, explaining to your future self why you made the decisions you did will be very helpful to stick to that plan. Below is a sample reference sheet I prepared for myself; I've also shared it electronically on Google Drive which may help you jump-start your own: valueofsimple.ca/RefSheet.html

Remember that your processes will have to fit *your* life. Rebalancing regularly is a good habit to have, but there's nothing special about January 1. Indeed, in my life I always find I'm short of time around the winter holidays so I set my annual check-up and rebalancing reminder to happen in March, when I have started to pull out all my financial statements to get ready for tax season anyway.

<u>Financial Planning Reference Sheet</u>

Name: John Robertson

Prepared: April 27, 2014 (age 34)

<u>Asset Allocation</u>

My target asset allocation is:

<u>Category</u>	<u>Product</u>	<u>Weighting & Tolerance</u>
(Canadian) Bonds	XQB in TFSA and RRSP, high-interest savings accounts in non-registered	Age - 20 (14% ± 5%)
Canadian Equity	XIC	33% of equities 28.7% ± 5% of overall
US Equity	VTI in RRSP, VUN in TFSA and non-registered	33% of equities 28.7% ± 5% of overall
International Equity	XEF	33% of equities 28.6% ± 5% of overall
* RESP, kept separate from retirement portfolio	TD e-series, split 25% into each of bonds, Canadian, US, and international equity	
Emergency Fund (Savings)	High interest savings account	Fixed, $4,000, not included in above percentages.

Also see spreadsheet at
https://docs.google.com/spreadsheet/ccc?key=0AktN0CUf4uaVdFBL

b09DVklHRm5fUVFYeWxObGlxSVE

[link or refer to your own rebalancing spreadsheet]

The reasons I chose this:

I am young with many years before retirement, and have a few years of service in a defined benefit pension plan. I have no upcoming major expenses, and am comfortable deferring any or reducing my budget if stock markets perform poorly. I have lived through the 2008/2009 stock crash, and know that though it caused some emotional stress, I was able to stick to my plan and stay invested. I have high confidence in my ability to stick to the plan if/when there is future market volatility and/or a crash.

Plan: I will review my allocation every year in March. As I make new contributions I will adjust my purchases to bring my portfolio back in line. If any component is off by more than 5% I will sell and repurchase other assets as needed.

If stock markets crash by more than 25%, I will view that as an opportunity and attempt to increase my savings rate, and am open to even investing my emergency fund. I will not adjust my plan for any other fluctuations in market prices, and even then will not make extreme deviations from my plan.

My allocation will become slightly more conservative over time, in accordance with the age-based rule above.

Rebalancing:

I will rebalance: a little with each purchase, with a pause to evaluate and rebalance once per year (March). I will rebalance *ad hoc* whenever my target allocations are off by more than 5%.

Account Allocation:

I will contribute my savings in this priority:

1. $2,500 to my daughter's RESP in January of every year.
2. Then contribute to my TFSA until that year's contribution room is used (currently $5,500/yr).
3. After that contribute to my RRSP (2014 contribution room: $2,700 due to pension adjustment).

4.   Then contribute to a non-registered account with any remaining savings, if there are any.

Because of my pension adjustment at my current job, and many years of university where I did not build RRSP room, my available tax shelter is smaller than the average Canadian my age. I will have to use my non-registered accounts and track capital gains accordingly.

I will use US-listed ETFs within my RRSP to maximize the tax benefit, however, I am most comfortable seeing each account as a fractal miniature of my overall, so I will maintain the same allocation balance in each, even if that may not be the most optimal configuration.

<u>Savings Plan:</u>

I project that I will need to save: $10,000 per year in 2014 dollars. I will increase my savings rate each year by 2% to keep pace with inflation, until my 5-year review.

This is based on the assumption that I will need $45,000 in annual retirement income (in 2014 dollars). I used a spreadsheet calculator tool at http://www.holypotato.net/?p=1243 to come up with these estimates. My assumptions include:

Inflation 2%, bond return 2.5%, stock return 8.5%; that I will get 80% of the maximum CPP, and full OAS at age 67; that I will have $9,000 in annual pension income; that I will retire at age 65 and need my savings to support me until age 95; that I will skip savings for 2 years on the assumption that I will have another child.

I will review my actual savings versus planned savings each year, and review my planned savings and assumptions versus reality every 5 years, with entries in my Google calendar for 2019, 2024 already set up.

Record-Keeping

I highly recommend creating a spreadsheet to track your investments. **For tax purposes you will need one for non-registered accounts**. It's not required for registered accounts like TFSAs and RRSPs, but you're always welcome to track your progress. Here's how you can set it up:

Date	Fund name/symbol	Price/unit	Units Purchased	Fees	Total Purchase	Notes
1/28/11	Can Index TDB900	Formula: =total/units purchased $21.07	35.60	0	$750	First investment with TD!
Etc.						

You can create a separate sheet (or separate section in each sheet) for each fund you have to make adding the totals easier when the time comes[65]. I have a spreadsheet modeled on how your capital gains will eventually be reported in your Schedule 3, available at http://www.holypotato.net/?p=1274

When you sell a fund, you'll need to know the average price paid per unit (or your adjusted cost base: "ACB"). You can find that by adding up all the units purchased, and the total price paid, and dividing price by units. For mutual funds, you will often find that since you can buy in any dollar amount you will often get fractions of a unit (e.g. here 35.60 units), and the price per unit may come out to an amount that's more precise than just pennies. Simply keep the extra digits until the end of your calculation (using the spreadsheet to do the math for you will make this automatic), and then round to the nearest penny when you do your taxes.

Your ACB gets a little more complicated if you've bought and sold, or if you received distributions that are "return of capital" or "capital gains", which can act as modifiers to decrease or increase your cost basis, respectively. Starting with good record-keeping is going to make tax time much easier for you.

---

[65] A hint: *do not* just intermingle your transactions by date. It will make it harder to sort things out later (but even then, some record-keeping is better than none).

Selling

To put it simply, selling works just like buying but in reverse. For mutual funds you just choose how much you would like to sell (in either units or dollars), and enter the order. For ETFs, you will enter a sell order (and your limit becomes the ask price). It will take 2 business days for your order to settle, so you won't be able to withdraw cash right away, but you will be able to purchase other ETFs (because those purchases will also take 2 days to settle – though note that different countries can have different holidays if you're buying and selling on different exchanges – you can always wait for the first trade to settle before placing another to be safe).

To then get your cash out and spend it is very straightforward with Tangerine or TD if you have an associated chequing account with them: just do an internal transfer, then pay bills, write a cheque, or withdraw as you ordinarily would from the chequing account. For Questrade, or the other options if you don't have an associated chequing account, you will need to set up an electronic funds transfer (the same three letters as ETF but note the order) to your chequing account at your bank.

Remember for regular cash or margin accounts (non-registered) that when you sell something you will have to report the capital gain (or loss) on your taxes that year.

Automation

It comes by many names: paying yourself first, spending the rest, or preauthorized purchase plans, but the idea boils down to the same thing. Automate your saving and investing so it's easier to stick to your plan and invisible to you. With mutual funds at Tangerine or TD you can pull money from your chequing account on a regular basis (weekly, biweekly, or monthly) and have it invested in your fund(s) of choice. For ETFs you may have to purchase manually after the automatic transfer of cash is made.

I quite recommend automatic contributions to your TFSA, RRSP, and then non-registered if those fill up. Remember though that you have limited room in your tax-sheltered accounts. For automatic contributions I would ensure that the monthly contribution is less than $1/12$ of your annual contribution room. That may mean adjusting your RRSP contributions every year, and your TFSA ones each time the government adjusts the annual contribution room.

Automatic contributions are an often-recommended and highly effective way to stick to a savings plan, and the behavioural reason is clear: our spending is often like a gas, expanding to fill the available volume. If your savings and long-term investments are taken out of your chequing account automatically as your paycheque arrives, you will quite likely find a way to live on the remaining amount. If you cut back on frivolous spending as part of your financial plan, you may not even notice the change in your quality of life as some spending may have been unconscious. When you try to put away whatever is left at the end of the month instead, you may find that unplanned or unconscious spending has eaten into your savings.

Even if you don't want to go into full automation – for instance if your HR department is staffed by flying monkeys who routinely delay posting your paycheque, and any automated transactions from your bank account may risk a bounced cheque or overdraft – you can semi-automate through calendar reminders to keep you on plan. I love Google Calendar for its ability to quickly create recurring events; the big benefit though is that I can also set them up to send me an email reminder. I can paste into the description field instructions to my future self. Some good reminders to set up include an annual rebalancing, to check your online statements at tax time, to contribute to your accounts. Here are some sample calendar reminders that you may find useful:

- March 15 every year: check accounts and rebalance if necessary. The description includes the file name for my Excel rebalancing spreadsheet to help me find it on my computer.

- January 2 every year: contribute to TFSA as new room just became available. Reminder to contribute to child's RESP, at least until government matching is maxed out.

- April 30 every year: reminder of tax deadline, and to invest tax refund. A reminder to update my 3-page summary from page 125 with my updated RRSP contribution room details.

- June 1 every year: a note-to-self that by this point the savings plan should have maxed out the RESP and TFSA contributions, so time to move on to RRSP or non-registered accounts.

Most of those dates are completely arbitrary and up to you. Try to make them fit your own life and plan: it's not super-critical which day of the year you rebalance as long as you do it regularly – roughly once per year is just an approximate rule-of-thumb. If your work and family keeps you busy near the new year, then put it in the late summer when things are calmer; I like to do it at tax time when I will have all my statements out anyway and my mind is fully in money mode. Use whatever works best for you and will make it easiest for you to stick to your plan.

Oh, and despite the media blitz that happens every February, RRSP "season" isn't really a big deal. You can contribute any day of the year, the deadline is just for whether you can claim it against one year's taxes or the one following. A more successful approach in my mind is to ignore all that last-minute stress, and go with a steady monthly contribution year-round. When you're 75 and spending that money you'll care whether it's there *at all* far more than whether the tax deduction was taken a year later. You can even fill out some forms with your employer to reduce the amount of tax taken off your paycheque each period so you don't have to wait for your refund to come in at the end of the year – which will also help remove the temptation to spend the refund.

With a good process in place – automation, reminder/summary sheets, rebalancing spreadsheet tools, calendar reminders, and uncomplicated choices and allocations – you hopefully won't need to work too hard to retain any of the specialized knowledge here. You can do all the hard stuff and make the major decisions while it's all fresh in your mind and the book is in front of you, then set it up to be as easy as possible for your future self to follow-through and stick to your plan.

> Set up a plan, put it into practice, and stick to it! Keep it **simple** yet **effective**: an emergency fund for the short term and just four funds will cover your bases for the long term. Keep your costs reasonably low. Rebalance when necessary, but not constantly. Automation can help you stick to your plan.

Burrowing Deep

Now to discuss some of the special situations, more advanced topics, and eternal debates. These include how to leave an existing advisor, consider the balance between investing and paying down your mortgage faster, taming the need to tinker, more discussions on tax – including a new metaphor for the RRSP – and how joint accounts work, important bits on your monthly statements, and some final words on process and expected value.

John Robertson

Taming the Need to Tinker

We are constantly bombarded by non-actionable noise (often called "financial news") urging us to invest one way or the other, to buy or to sell. When markets roil and crash this can spread from the business section to the front page, water-cooler talk, and even dinner conversations. Fear is a powerful emotion, and can demand our focus: many investors may go months without paying attention to "boring" business news or the state of the market, but when it looks like the wheels are coming off we can't help but worry and obsess.

Knowing how you will really react to seeing up to half of your portfolio's value disappear is nearly impossible until it happens. You can imagine it all you like, but it's much easier to dissociate your emotions about a decline when you're devising your plan and considering your risk tolerance one calm Saturday afternoon than it is to have lived with week after week of new record lows being set, and seeing pessimism everywhere you look.

It is at this point that the urge to tinker may be strongest, as people make the disastrous call to "sell everything!" so they can "stop the bleeding" and get back to sleep at night. Let's look again at that chart of long-term returns on page 11.

136

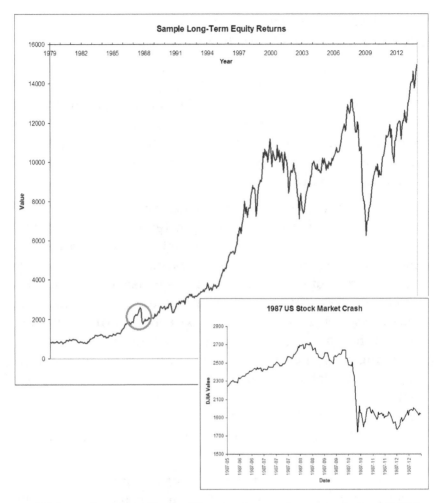

Sample Long-Term Equity Returns

1987 US Stock Market Crash

Did you notice the major stock market crash in 1987? I've magnified it in the insert. That was known as "Black Monday" and was a major deal at the time. Stocks declined by 22% in a single day. But in the long-term view it's barely noticeable as a blip.

At the time a market crash seems catastrophic: it's affecting everything you own, everything you've saved up to that point, and it looks to be gone in a flash. If you wanted to sell your stocks and take the money out the next day to spend it, you couldn't, at least not all of what you thought you could the day before. That can be downright terrifying and gut-wrenching.

But if it's a long-term investment then *you weren't going to do that anyway.* And looking back on it from the future, it's a blip you can barely notice. And that's just looking at what the index did on its own. If you add in the fact that you're saving regularly each year then it looks even better, as you get more units per dollar invested when markets are lower.

Large market crashes are good opportunities to buy more, through rebalancing and/or temporarily increasing your savings rate. Following through on that can be very hard to do at the time. The news may be full of people predicting doom and gloom and further market losses. Over the short term those predictions may even be correct, which helps give the next set of warnings further weight in your mind. Your friends and family may be wringing their hands; you may even be losing sleep at night if you let it get under your skin. This is the point where investors often work against themselves: by not buying more and rebalancing – or worse yet, selling and crystallizing the losses – they leave their carefully laid out plans just when those plans would most help them.

I can look back at what I was writing during the 2008/2009 market crash and I see that indeed I had the same concerns and fears. It was a legitimately scary time, with US banks being declared insolvent and taken over by the government, while Canadian banks were issuing shares to shore up their own capital bases, and taking back-door bailouts from our government through CMHC. But despite the angst I felt at the time, I separated my emotions from my actions and was buying more equities all the way down in the crash, rebalancing my savings according to the plan. Indeed, I even put off major purchases to increase my savings rate and buy more equities.

For people who are still in the savings and investment phase of their lives, lower stock prices are a *good* thing.

It's fine to feel things and talk through them with supportive friends; you can't turn yourself into a robot or completely shut out the news. Success will come based on your *actions*, so despite any panic you feel at the time, remember to act according to your plan.

Of course, if you don't have several years to wait for the markets to recover, then a market crash can be even worse. That is why most asset allocation rules-of-thumb incorporate your age: as you get closer to needing the money (i.e. retirement) your asset allocation should get more conservative.

Similar to the urge to tinker or run in the midst of a crash, there is a tendency to over-weight equities after a period of stock markets performing well. That is also a bad time to change the plan, as you can fool yourself into thinking that your risk tolerance is higher than it really is when equities don't *look* risky or volatile.

These types of common errors are why many investors get personal returns that lag those of what buy-and-hold investors in the same funds get.

Another common need to tinker comes not from moves in the market, but from the indexing approach itself. It seems almost absurd that a large collection of broadly diversified companies has a better chance of providing higher returns than picking a few really promising stocks, either by paying a professional to pick them or picking some yourself. The absurdity is even greater when you consider that most popular indexes were never *intended* to be investment products, but started as a way to report an "average" figure for how the stock market was doing.

The most straightforward argument is that the overall market is the sum of all investors: so the average investor must get the average return, less fees. Cutting your fees down by investing in passive index products will maximize your expected return. But *some* investors will do better than average, and the lure of that possibility can be irresistible, even if it's unlikely. *Setting out* to get the average market return is a tough concept to get on board with, even if doing so actually makes you an above-average investor who can more easily avoid the emotional foibles of the masses.

Even after you accept that indexing is a great way to go, the urge to *attempt* to out-perform, whether by timing the market, over-fitting your asset allocation model with 20 different sub-sector ETFs, or just picking stocks that you have "gut feelings" about can be overwhelming.

My best advice is to get control of your emotions and your urges, set up a simple, easy-to-follow investment plan (like that laid out in the previous chapters), and then tune out the noise of day-to-day market fluctuations and specific stock stories.

If you can't do that, then the next best thing is to tame the need to tinker through an approach known as **core-and-explore**. Set up *most* of your portfolio in a passively indexed fashion. Then set aside some portion – that you can afford to lose – to scratch your tinkering itch. Whether that's allocating 5% to gold and precious metals, and another 5% to emerging markets, or taking 15% and buying the three stocks that represent your best investing ideas and which you just can't help but attempt to invest in, "playing" with 5-15% is not likely to hurt you too badly[66]. And if it will help you stay on the wagon for the lion's share of your portfolio then some good will come of it.

---

[66] Greatly depending on your individual circumstances, of course.

Behavioural factors can be the most important determinants of long-term success. Every move away from a simple, effective plan risks costly errors, but sticking to a plan can be hardest when it is most important. Consider implementing methods to tame the need to tinker.

Breaking Up Is Surprisingly Easy to Do

If you already have an advisor (or a commissioned salesperson who you refer to as an advisor) and they focus on picking expensive, actively managed mutual funds for you – and are not producing value for money – then you may wish to fire your advisor and become a self-directed, do-it-yourself investor using what you've learned in this book.

Approaching them to leave may be awkward, especially as many advisors build very personal rapports that don't seem like you're in a salesperson-customer relationship. The point-of-view is so deep that many don't call it "switching accounts" or even "leaving" but rather "breaking up."

Indeed, the hidden nature of mutual fund fees is a clever bit of social engineering, as this hides the commercial aspect of the relationship, and makes it less likely that a customer will consider the potential conflicts-of-interest or critically question the advisor. Once your eyes have been opened to how your salesperson is compensated, and how large an effect a fee of a percentage or two can have on your long-term wealth then hard feelings may result: the monetary aspect becomes a "betrayal" of what many had previously (subconsciously) considered something akin to friendship. So, it's time to leave and set off to invest on your own.

If you attempt to confront your advisor then they will have an opportunity to try to dissuade you from an index approach, or attempt a guilt-trip. There are a number of common arguments advisors use. These often have logical fallacies, or sound good but aren't backed up in the data. Note that because they are primarily in a sales role, your advisor will likely make these appear compelling (at least as long as you are within their reality distortion field and don't have the time to research or critically evaluate the argument and evidence).

If you're about to switch to passive index investing, you may find that the goalposts can be moved by your salesperson, with the pitch that perhaps they can deliver "absolute returns" or "lower volatility" than an index approach. That can be a persuasive argument, as can the thought that some human agency is tending to your portfolio. Even though humans make all kinds of critical errors, it can be a reassuring thought next to the notion that you've handed over your investments to a passive sampling of global capitalism.

One fact I like to remind people who are having trouble leaving their commission-based advisors of is that, by and large, an advisor gets paid for being a good salesperson and not for being a good stock-picker. Their arguments will sound persuasive if they are good at their job. Remember that many pension funds have looked at the evidence and decided to follow an indexing approach themselves.

Some common arguments they may try to sway you with include:

- That a skilled advisor can choose the portion of funds that will, through luck or skill, beat the index net of fees.

  o The evidence shows that this is usually not the case.

- That active management can help avoid losses and protect your money in a market crash.

  o Funds underperformed their benchmarks just as much in 2008/2009 as they did in other periods; active management if anything encouraged more selling out at the bottom and delayed buying in as markets recovered.

- That you wouldn't want some mindless index algorithm in control of your money, like a driverless car – an appeal to control.

  o Though having a human in charge of your funds feels comforting, it is a demonstrably weaker strategy, with higher costs, salaries to pay, and more room to make mistakes.

- That people who use advisors are wealthier.

  o This is true but is because people who have money are more likely to go to an advisor than because advisors *make* people wealthy. Think about private jets: people who use private jets are more likely to be wealthier, but that's not because private jets are generating the wealth.

- That they offer other services like planning.

  o This may be true, however many salespeople focus on investment product selection and do not provide their clients with comprehensive financial plans or other services like counselling through market turmoil – in other words, they are not offering value for money. The big banks are particularly bad at this as you may never see the same person twice. Be sure that you are getting value for your money: you can invest in low-cost funds, pay by the hour for a planner to fill in the other services, and still come out with significant savings.

Fortunately, breaking up is surprisingly easy to do. Once you make the decision, you never have to see your advisor again: there is an established process in Canada to have your new bank or brokerage "pull" your investments over from your old advisor. You can elect to do this in the process of opening your new account by just checking a few boxes and filling in your old account information in the application form, or contact a representative to help you do it after your account is open. If your old firm charges a fee to transfer out and/or cancel your accounts, then your new firm may pay this for you. Be sure to ask about that with the new firm if that applies to you.

Keep in mind that the firm you are moving to wants your business, so they will help make the transition as easy as possible for you.

Transferring directly from your old firm, directed by your new firm, is the way to go especially if you have an RRSP or some other registered funds. If you attempt to move funds yourself, you may accidentally withdraw from a registered account and face a tax bill and lose the contribution room. A proper account transfer is the only way to do it.

For the TFSA however, the situation can be a bit different. Some companies charge a transfer-out fee (up to $150 in some cases), but often do not charge a fee to withdraw cash on your own. Because you get TFSA contribution room back in the following calendar year you can do what's known as the "TFSA shuffle": withdraw from your old TFSA, hold the cash/investments in your non-registered accounts until the year ends, and then contribute to your new TFSA in January.

If you have funds with deferred sales charges (DSCs) then you may need to take more care in your separation. These fees can run up to 7% or more if you sell earlier than the fund company allows. Given the magnitude of this, it may be worth waiting for a few years to ride out the DSCs, even if you're paying higher ongoing MERs. If you ask, your old advisor will provide a table indicating which funds have DSCs and the terms associated with them, which can help you plan your exit. For instance, if you're allowed to sell up to 20% of your funds per year without paying a fee, then do so, and work your way out. If the DSC is comparable to the MER – as can happen with DSCs that slowly get reduced rather than sharply ending – then it may make sense to just rip the bandaid off and get into low-cost products.

Mortgage or Invest?

Whether to use extra cash in your budget to pay down the mortgage or invest is an extremely common question – discussions seem to appear every year around "RRSP season." Unfortunately there isn't a hard-and-fast rule or answer other than "it depends." It depends in part on your risk tolerance, your expectation for investment returns compared to your mortgage rate, and the likelihood you will upgrade/move up or remortgage to spend on "stuff" if your mortgage was paid down.

A common answer is to "do both!" with the suggestion that you contribute to your RRSP with your savings, and use your tax refund to pay down the mortgage. If it weren't for that quirk of the RRSP people would not gravitate nearly so much to the "do both" answer. I have never, ever seen someone say "take two-thirds of your money, put it in your TFSA, and put the other third towards paying down your mortgage," even though that would be equivalent to the RRSP "do both" answer.

My general answer is *also* to *do both*, but I think my reasons are a little more robust.

Here is my reasoning: many of the factors that make the answer a wishy-washy "it depends" are common to pretty much everyone: mortgage rates are very similar (especially now, after five years of uniformly low rates) as is the expected investment return. You will most likely make more in equities than you will by avoiding interest on your mortgage, even though *avoiding* interest is an entirely after-tax return. The marginal tax rate will vary a bit, but that's not a huge factor, especially if you are able to invest in a TFSA or RRSP. Yet if these factors are so common, the answer should be standardized, rather than a matter of opinion and eternal debate. Risk tolerance and how you feel about the debt versus diversification are important too, but not the only factors. When there isn't a strong reason to pick one option over the other in situations like this, I like to split the difference – get a bit of the best of both.

If you focus exclusively on your mortgage early in your investing years you will have to save more later in life to make up for it. And no matter how much you pay down your principal early, if you have a job loss or emergency your bank will still demand the future mortgage payments get made – you don't get to skip them based on your previous good behaviour[67]. That means you'll need the flexibility of some kind of investment or emergency fund, so you need to put some money aside from your mortgage, even if doing so would not be optimal from a returns or sleeping-at-night perspective. However, it doesn't really make much sense to hold large amounts of bonds or GICs to earn some interest when you are paying more on a mortgage.

My suggested compromise is to recognize that there are benefits to each approach, that it is difficult to optimize, and so to split the difference by doing a bit of both. Take your investment allocation and put the equity portion into equities, and the bond portion towards paying off your mortgage. If you have enough savings to fill your TFSA and RRSP, then redirect the rest back towards your mortgage; if you use up all your pre-payment privileges then invest. For example, if you're 35

---

[67] Some mortgages can have "payment vacation" or "skip-a-payment" privileges in the terms, but these are almost never flexible enough to cover a prolonged job loss. Do not "burn your mortgage" to the exclusion of all else, as there can be a lot of value in liquid funds you can access in an emergency, on top of the other benefits to investing over your lifetime rather than waiting for the mortgage to be paid off first.

and would want 25% of your assets to be in bonds, then put 25% of your savings towards extra principal payments on the mortgage, and the rest towards investing[68]. If you find mortgage rates increasing in the future, leading to higher monthly mortgage costs, then you may want to start selling some of your investments to put a lump sum payment towards your mortgage at renewal – this is where the flexibility of the TFSA is especially useful.

Using the TFSA or a non-registered account is a key part of the split-the-difference strategy: if you find yourself in that unfortunate situation of needing to sell investments to pay the mortgage, then having them locked up in an RRSP will take away some flexibility.

Of course if you're more risk-averse, then putting a higher priority on the mortgage pay-down may suit you better. If you're more risk-tolerant, then you may not want to pay the mortgage off any faster than the original amortization and instead direct everything to investing.

-----

[68] Note that this will break part of the benefit of a balanced portfolio in that you will see the value of your investments swing with more volatility as your mortgage paydown isn't included in your brokerage balance. Approach with caution and awareness of how you will respond to volatility.

A Twist: Currency Neutral Funds

In *Step 4c: Investing with TD Direct Investing* on page 96 I just mentioned four TD e-series funds, but you may notice that on the complete list of e-series funds on TD's website that for US and international equity funds there are at least two versions: one denominated in Canadian dollars, and another one also in Canadian dollars but called "currency neutral." Many ETF providers also have currency neutral versions of their funds. These currency neutral funds attempt to eliminate the change in valuation between the Canadian dollar and the US dollar (or, for the international fund, the Canadian dollar and a basket of foreign currencies like the pound, euro, yen, and Australian dollar).

If you've ever gone cross-border shopping in the US then you're probably well aware of the exchange rate, and also that it changes over time. Those changes in the value of the Canadian dollar relative to other currencies don't only affect the price you pay for goods, but also for stocks. If the US S&P 500 index goes nowhere for a year, but the Canadian dollar goes up by 5%, then your investment in US stocks would actually be worth 5% less if you had to sell. Vice-versa, if the Canadian dollar goes down that would increase your returns. The currency neutral investment would only give you (*in theory*) whatever the S&P 500 returned, without the added effect of the changing Canadian dollar.

I say in theory because this currency hedging usually costs something, and that cost is not counted in the MER listed. It costs up to 1% per year for the hedging: that cost appears in what is known as "tracking error." Because currency fluctuations are usually manageable in the long term, and because one direction of currency fluctuations (the Canadian dollar weakening) is *good* for your foreign investments, it's usually recommended that long-term investors not bother with currency neutral funds.

However, in the short term changes in the dollar can be almost as extreme as changes in stock prices, so in some situations it may be worthwhile to consider the currency neutral version of the funds. Mostly, that would be where you have an intermediate time horizon: long enough to still maintain an equity exposure, but short enough that currency moves may not average out. My rule-of-thumb would be about 3-7 years – and you don't have to make your entire portfolio currency neutral.

A Twist: US ETFs

The US and Canada have a tax treaty: the impact for you is, briefly, that the US will withhold 15% of any dividends going to Canadian investors on US equities. However, the RRSP (but not the TFSA) is exempted from this withholding tax. That means there is a slight advantage to holding US equity ETFs in your RRSP, and buying those from American providers in US dollars[69].

Remember that there is value in simplicity. Taking the first steps in this book – getting started with investing, and investing in ETFs yourself to control costs – has a large impact on your results compared to a more typical actively managed mutual fund, which might have a MER 2 percentage points higher. Trying to perfectly optimize your holdings across your RRSP and other accounts, converting currencies, and holding US-domiciled ETFs to minimize the US withholding tax adds a rather large amount of complexity to shave a much more modest amount off your costs – a savings of about 0.3% on just one component of your portfolio[70], for just the portion in an RRSP. Keep this message of simplicity in mind as you read this chapter, and feel free to skip it if at any point it sounds overwhelming.

Vanguard is the leader south of the border, and the two main funds to look at are **VOO** and **VTI**, both trading on the NYSEARCA exchange (in TD just choose "US" for

---

[69] The reason it has to be a US ETF is that a Canadian fund will pay the withholding tax on your behalf before it gets to the shelter of your RRSP.

[70] Calculated as a 15% withholding tax on a dividend yield of approximately 2%.

the market drop-down; in Questrade the symbols without any suffix will bring them up). As a small bonus, the MER is slightly lower on the American version of the ETFs (0.05% for VOO vs. 0.10% for XUS; 0.05% for VTI vs. 0.15% for VUN). Owning these US-listed funds in your RRSP will help you avoid the US withholding tax on the dividends.

However, these US-listed funds have to be purchased in US dollars (USD). There is a cost to convert your Canadian dollars: TD charges roughly 1.5% on top of the current exchange rate, and Questrade 2%, though this conversion will happen automatically once you purchase a USD-denominated fund. You will make this back in an RRSP through the tax savings in a couple of years so it's likely worthwhile even at that premium, but those high fees do take the shine off this strategy. There is a way to convert more cheaply by using the DLR and DRL.U ETFs, both of which trade on the TSX (even though one is denominated in US dollars), though this will involve paying fixed commission costs. The process is a little involved.

If you want to search online for more details, this process is known as "Norbert's gambit." One way to think about Norbert's gambit is to visualize the physical case: if you were in Windsor, Ontario and wanted some American dollars, you could go to your local bank and they would charge you a 2% premium for them – though the exchange rate might be at par, the bank would charge you $1.02 Canadian for each American dollar you bought. To avoid that, you could buy something that's easy to sell for a universal value on either side of the border – a gold coin, or a share of stock – with your Canadian dollars, walk across the bridge to Detroit, and sell it to get American dollars at the fair exchange rate, avoiding the bank's fees. That is pretty much what you'll do in

Norbert's gambit, but with units of an ETF, and you never have to leave your desk.

Horizons has created an ETF pair that just tracks the relative values of the Canadian and US dollars. Listed on the TSX, DLR can be purchased in (or sold for) Canadian dollars, at a price that is very close to the current fair exchange rate. The paired fund, DLR.U, can be exchanged for US dollars even though it also trades on the TSX. In brief, you will buy DLR with your Canadian dollars, which can be converted into DLR.U, which you sell in US dollars. Once you have USD in your account, you buy your US-listed ETF without having to pay the brokerage's currency exchange fee.

The only trick then is following the steps to be able to buy one and sell the other within your brokerage accounts. The main reason to convert your currency and buy a US-listed fund is to save on that withholding tax in an RRSP, so that is where the discussion will focus. However, Norbert's gambit can also be used to exchange funds in a non-registered account if you ever need to[71].

Norbert's Gambit for TD: At TD, you will have separate sub-accounts for your US-denominated and Canadian-denominated investments (for your RRSP as well as TFSA and non-registered). First, determine how much money you have available to invest in your desired US-listed ETF. Then, in the order entry → stocks page, get a quote on DLR trading on the Canadian exchange, and make sure that you have your CAD sub-account selected in the account drop-down (typically the account suffix for CAD RRSPs is –S). The *ask* price is the price we will have to pay per share, and because this is in TD I will also have to set aside $10 for commissions before figuring out how

---

[71] There's no reason to in the plans laid out here, however there can be lots of reasons you may find yourself with the need to cheaply convert large amounts of Canadian or US currency.

many units I can afford. The trade should happen almost instantly, as there is an active market in the DLR ETF, but will take two business days in Canada for the trade to settle.

Then, you call TD Direct Investing and ask a representative to "journal" your DLR units to your USD account (typically the suffix for your USD RRSP is –U). This may take another day for the units to appear in the account. Then, you can sell the paired DLR.U, and you'll have US dollars appear in your account. You'll be entering your order to sell at the *bid* price.

With USD in hand, you can purchase ETFs listed on the American exchanges, such as Vanguard's total stock market index (VTI).

At the end of the process, we'll have USD ready to buy a cheaper (and more tax-efficient in an RRSP) US-listed ETF such as VTI. To have converted cash to USD using the no-effort automatic conversion of the brokerage would have cost about 1.5–2% on top of the difference in value between the countries. By putting this effort in we paid about $0.02/unit in the "spread" (paying the ask, taking the bid in the transactions) plus $20 in extra commissions, which could represent hundreds of dollars in savings, depending on how much you have to convert. Though it was some work and effort[72], Norbert's gambit is usually worthwhile for converting large amounts. Of course the main question is whether to get into the level of effort of buying US-listed ETFs to save a few tenths of a percent in taxes on a portion of your portfolio in the first place.

To convert from USD back to CAD, simply go in the opposite order: buy DLR.U with the USD first, call the

---

[72] It took me about 25 minutes all told, though I was going slow, taking notes and screenshots.

broker to journal back to DLR in the CAD account, then sell the DLR units. In summary, at TD (and similar brokerages with a split CAD/USD sub-account structure):

1. Buy DLR in your CAD account. Wait 2 days.

2. Call the help line, ask an agent to "journal" DLR to DLR.U in your USD account.

3. Sell DLR.U, then buy VTI in your USD account.

Norbert's Gambit for Questrade: The first, one-time step in Questrade is to ensure that you have the correct option selected for how your trades settle – choose "trade currency" under "currency settlement", found in the Account Management page of MyQuestrade (RRSP and TFSA accounts only). Otherwise you will end up going through the process only to end up with USD that automatically get converted back to CAD before you can buy anything – paying the commissions and premium exchange rate for nothing. Beyond that, the steps are similar, except that the purchases are commission-free (but not the DLR.U sale), and there's only one sub-account for your RRSP. When you can call in (or use their online live support) to journal DLR to DLR.U, you don't need to move it between accounts, just from the CAD version to the USD version.

At what point that effort becomes worth it depends on how you value your time to go through the process versus the brokerage's instant conversion convenience. To pay one or two commissions (at Questrade the purchase side is free) and the very minor spread of the DLR ETF pair represents a fairly small cost, with a portion of it fixed. The economic break-even point is at roughly $1,400, and it becomes more worthwhile for larger amounts. Personally, I don't bother for conversions under about $5,000 (i.e. savings of ~$45) as I find it a hassle and I only convert every year or two anyway.

A Caution on Holidays: Most days of the year this procedure goes off without a hitch, however sometimes the behind-the-scenes machinery is important to keep in mind: ETFs and stocks have a 2-day period to "settle" trades. Because you're dealing with two countries, holidays don't always line up and the 2 days to settle can happen at different times. For instance, if you place this trade on the Friday before Canadian Thanksgiving, then your sale of DLR.U to create USD will take the holiday Monday off, and so settle on the following Wednesday (two business days). However, the US markets stay open that Monday, and your US ETF purchase will settle on Tuesday – a day before your USD are ready to cover it. You would be charged interest in that case for falling short, sometimes at credit-card like rates. Be sure to check for market holidays on both sides of the border before setting up the trade, or wait for each component to settle in turn.

Advanced Tax

Canada has a progressive taxation system, which means that we tax a higher proportion of every dollar earned when someone makes more money. Without getting too political, this makes a lot of sense: *life* puts a "tax" on earnings through the cost of basic necessities. As people make more, they have more income to spend on disposable items, so they also have the capacity to shoulder more of the tax burden.

The calculation behind progressive taxation is that there are tiers with different tax rates, or several "tax brackets." The details on the amount of tax and income thresholds for each tax bracket are available from the Canada Revenue Agency's (CRA) website[73]. I find that in books or websites explaining them, they are often presented in the same way the government does for calculation purposes:

- 15% on the first $45,916 of taxable income, +
- 20.5% on the next $45,915 of taxable income (on the portion of taxable income over $45,916 up to $91,831), +
- 26% on the next $50,522 of taxable income (on the portion of taxable income over $91,831 up to $142,353), +
- 29% on the next $60,447taxable income (on the portion of taxable income over $142,353 up to $202,800.), +
- 33% of taxable income over $202,800

---

[73] http://www.cra-arc.gc.ca/tx/ndvdls/fq/txrts-eng.html

These are just the income taxes sent to the federal government, so a similar table usually follows with different rates and income thresholds for your provincial income tax. This approach is both too complicated and too simple to capture the idea of tax brackets, so instead I would like to try to explain it graphically.

In the first image (next page), imagine that you are filling a bucket with money you earn. The bucket is divided into a portion the government keeps, and a portion you keep. Where that dividing line falls shifts ever closer to the middle as your income increases – as you get closer to the top of the bucket. At the very bottom, the government takes nothing, this is the "basic personal amount" that, instead of appearing as a 0% bracket in the standard table above, comes through as a tax credit everyone receives. As your earnings cross about[74] $10,000 you start paying at the lowest tax bracket. At that point the government is taking about 20% of each *new* dollar you earn, but that does not affect the untaxed first $10,000 or so you made. That continues as your income moves up – in the example I have put a "fill line" for someone with $70,000 of regular employment earnings – those last few thousand dollars earned were taxed at about 31%. However, if you look at the total dark grey shaded area on the left, which would be the total amount of tax payable, it averages out to closer to 20%.

---

[74] The basic personal amount is different federally and provincially, $11,635 for the federal amount and $10,171 for the Ontario amount in 2017. Hence the "about".

John Robertson

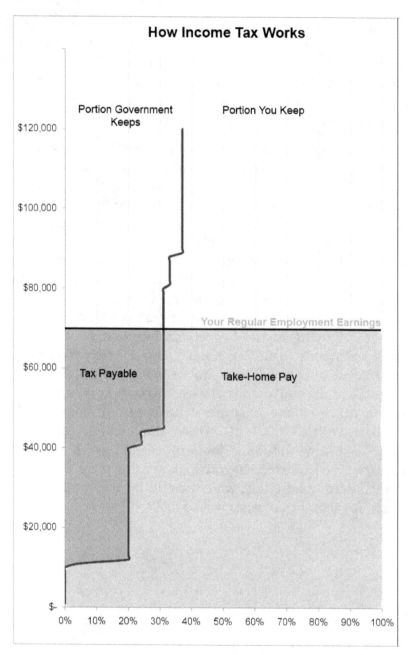

An illustration of progressive taxation, using rounded 2014 rates for Ontario and federal income tax. Note that that the real-life situation is more complicated than this, for instance this does not include the Ontario Health Premium or Ontario surtax, which *would make the marginal rate on incomes over about $88,000 exceed 43%, vs the 37% shown. The tax payable line has several small steps because the provincial and federal cut-offs are not quite the same.*

Your **marginal tax rate** is the percentage the government keeps on that last (or next) dollar of income. There is a lot of focus on marginal tax rate because it's what's important to consider for a lot of decision-making. For example, if you were trying to figure out what to do with some investments that had different tax efficiencies, or whether to contribute to an RRSP, then your marginal tax rate would be the critical factor. After all, your regular employment earnings will be there either way.

If, like many Canadians, you are employed by an employer, then they will give you a tax form called a T4 (and send a copy to the CRA) that will conveniently list all of your employment income, as well as some ancillary information[75] in numbered boxes that will streamline filing your taxes. One in particular will show how much tax has been withheld on your behalf through the year.

Going back to the example of someone making $70,000 per year, their total tax bill would be roughly $15,000. That is a lot of money to come up with every April, and many people might not think ahead to save up for the tax bill. To avoid a catastrophe, the government instead takes an amount off of each paycheque as a down-payment against your year-end tax bill. Ideally (from their point of view), they will withhold more than you will end up owing, and will make it up to you with a tax refund after filing – in addition to minimizing the number of people who don't pay their taxes, it provides you with an incentive to file your taxes on time. Filing, of course, being the process of filling out the forms each

---

[75] For example, how much you paid through a payroll deduction for transit passes, union dues, pension contributions, etc.

spring to calculate precisely what your income is, what credits and deductions you may have to reduce how much tax you must pay, and submitting that to the government.

Tax withheld is not such a difficult concept then, but it causes some problems because it's nearly invisible while refunds are highly visible. What ends up mattering the most to what you can spend and save in your life is how much tax you have to pay rather than how much is withheld through the year or refunded in the end. Where refunds can be particularly confusing is when it comes to RRSP contributions.

How RRSPs Work

Briefly, money contributed to an RRSP is saved *before tax*. That is, whatever amount you put into an RRSP gives you a "deduction" to remove that much from your income for the year. Because that money already had tax withheld on it through the year, it ends up increasing your refund after you file your taxes. The focus on the refund issue loses sight of how it is that RRSPs work: **they let your investments grow tax-free over time**, and shift the taxation to the future. So let's modify the bucket-filling visual metaphor from before into the second image, and with a touch of sci-fi, allow me to explain it in a new way.

Let's start from someone making $70,000 as a base salary again, but now they make a $5,000 RRSP contribution. The RRSP contribution (top dark bar in the second image) escapes tax in the working years (left side) by sneaking out through a parallel dimension called a "tax shelter" by some (or "registered account"). There it grows fat, with no tax on ongoing growth, awaiting your signal to re-enter our reality when you are safely in your retirement years. When you do withdraw the money, it then comes in as taxable income (medium grey portion of RRSP funds on the right, future half of the figure). Like many people, you may be in a lower tax bracket in retirement (starting further down on the figure), so the RRSP provides an added benefit in that you'll end up paying less tax, and deferring the bill until later.

So the whole tax refund thing is just a consequence of that sci-fi time-shifting that the RRSP allows: you already had tax withheld on that income before it was lost to the RRSP time vortex. With your income reduced (in the present-day timestream) by the RRSP contribution, the government gives that tax withheld back to you as a tax refund. But it's best to **consider a portion of that RRSP contribution as the government's portion that they will take back** – when it comes out of the RRSP tax-shelter parallel dimension, they will take their cut then. You will not be able to spend every dollar sitting within your RRSP, some will be lost to tax. Notice that in the graphic: the RRSP contribution included the part on the left side of the bucket, the government's portion.

For simplicity the figure doesn't show the RRSP contribution growing between the working and retirement years, but that's just what it will do if you invest it for the long term – and it will grow *tax-free* while it's in that "parallel dimension." Note that while *withdrawals* are taxed, the *growth* isn't, as the government's portion grows at the same rate to pay the future taxes (imagine that bar at double the height across the full width of the future bucket).

If you're in the same tax bracket at retirement, the RRSP is still providing a major benefit in letting your investments grow tax-free (exactly equal to the benefit of the TFSA in that case) – indeed, this is the main benefit of the RRSP, and withdrawing at a lower rate than you contributed is just a bonus (or a penalty if your tax bracket increases).

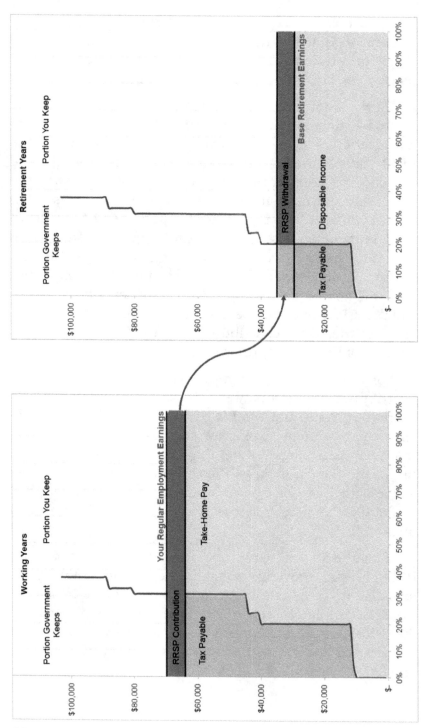

Facing page: A simple view of how RRSPs work. No tax is taken off of the amount contributed (working years, left). Contributions can grow tax-free over time, and then withdrawn at some point in the future (retirement years, right) – ideally when you will be in a lower tax bracket. At this point it is counted as income and tax is taken off (medium grey shaded region of RRSP withdrawal).

If you expect to be in a higher tax bracket in the future than you are now (for instance, if you're early into what you hope will become a high-paying career) then you may wish to hang on to your RRSP room until you're in a higher tax bracket, particularly if you have TFSA room to use instead. However, the benefit of tax-free compounding can outweigh a small difference in tax rates separated by many years, so you'll have to do some math to see if a non-registered (taxable) account would be better if you expect your tax rate to increase in the near future. And don't forget that when it's a close call, an RRSP also frees you of the burden to track and report the gains on your investments.

When withdrawing money from your RRSP, your bank will issue you a T4RSP – analogous to the T4 received from your employer – reporting the amount of the withdrawal, which will add to your income. Similar to employment earnings, tax will be withheld from your withdrawal, with the rate depending on how much you withdraw. If you convert your RRSP to an RRIF[76] then the withdrawals count as pension income rather than ordinary income, which gets you a small tax credit.

Comparatively, the TFSA is a simpler concept: you take your money (your *after tax* take-home pay) and put it

---

[76] RRIF stands for Registered Retirement Income Fund, basically an RRSP that forces you to withdraw a minimum amount each year. You must convert your RRSP into an RRIF by age 71, and can opt to do it before that. The minimums are available at: http://www.cra-arc.gc.ca/E/pub/tp/ic78-18r6/ic78-18r6-e.html

in a special account where further investment returns and interest are not taxed. The in/out contribution rules can be a source of confusion but it is overall much simpler.

Taxable Investment Income: If you can't shelter all of your investments from taxes in your TFSA or RRSP, then you'll have to include certain components of your non-registered investment returns in your taxable income. For savings accounts and GICs you will receive a T5 slip for any interest income over $50/yr, which makes filing your taxes just as easy as copying the amounts in the boxes to your tax software. If you don't cross the $50 threshold you still have to report and pay tax on the interest income, but it's up to you to add up your statements to report it. Yes, even the $2 in interest you got from your chequing account over the year.

For mutual funds and ETFs, you will have several kinds of income. Dividends, interest, or other distributions will be reported on T3 or T5 slips, which your brokerage will send to you. Capital gains are your responsibility to track, and that tracking was covered in detail earlier (*Record-Keeping*, page 128).

Capital gains can be confusing in some situations. Only half of your net capital gains are added to your income for the year (making them tax efficient), and you can carry any net capital losses forward to reduce future capital gains or revise past tax returns up to three years in the past to reduce past capital gains.

Perhaps the most confusing component is the **superficial loss** rule: if you sell an investment at a loss, you can't use the loss to reduce your capital gains if you bought the same investment within 30 days (either before or after), instead you just continue to follow the adjusted cost until you finally sell the security without re-buying it, or sell it with a capital gain (there is *no* parallel "superficial gain" rule). Basically, this is to prevent people from temporarily selling something that is down and claiming the loss on their taxes if they were to continue to hold it for the long term (people are always looking for ways to reduce their current taxes).

If you don't sell then you do not have capital gains (or losses) to report on your taxes. That is, capital gains (and losses) can be *deferred* until you do sell. The notable exception is a "deemed disposition" where you may still own something, but had a transaction that counts as a sale. The most common case of this is when you do an in-kind contribution of a fund or ETF to your TFSA or RRSP: once it goes into the tax shelter, you will have to pay tax on any gains made up to that point (though you cannot claim any losses).

Joint accounts are the final point of common confusion. The portion of the gains in a joint account is supposed to be allocated according to who owns that portion of the underlying asset, which the CRA will determine based on who put the money in. You may consider the money "ours, equally" but the CRA may say it's "100% hers" based on where the funds in the joint account came from. A consequence is that you can't just arbitrarily change who the owner is to put your dividends and capital gains into the name of your lower-income spouse each year.

If you share assets with a partner (whether through joint accounts or individual ones), and you wish to have the non-registered investments taxed in the hands of the lower-income partner, then that partner has to contribute the funds. You can't just have the higher-income partner deposit some money in the lower-income partner's account – the CRA could decide that the "beneficial owner" is the higher-income partner in that case and allocate the tax burden (and marginal tax rate) accordingly. One strategy is to have the higher-income partner pay more of the household expenses so that the lower-income partner can invest proportionately more of their income. Another strategy is to set up a loan between partners (and yes, you have to pay each other interest), but is getting beyond the scope here.

Reading Your Statements

There are several basic documents you will have available to you for your investing accounts. Each provider will present them in slightly different way, but the basic information will be pretty much the same. For each of these documents, most firms (including Tangerine, TD, and Questrade) will give you separate copies for each of your accounts (non-registered, TFSA, RRSP, RESP).

Trade confirmations will detail the individual buy/sell transactions you make, including the total price paid/received, the number of units traded, and any fees or commissions. They can be a convenient way to track each transaction for your taxable account, but the information will be repeated on your monthly statement. If you have a dividend reinvestment program on any of your holdings, then the purchases made through that will not generate trade confirmations. Note that the default is for TD e-series to reinvest any dividends.

Monthly statements usually detail the total value of each of your accounts, with some indication of your asset breakdown and how much cash you have available. You will have a collection of all transactions through the month, which includes the purchases and sales that would lead to trade confirmations as well as any dividends and reinvested dividends. You will even see cash transfers in or out of the account and foreign exchange transactions.

For the holdings view you will generally see a list of your holdings, and a column for your "**book value**" and "**market value**." These represent how much you paid for each security as well as how much it was worth at the time the statement was prepared, respectively. Note that the book value is usually *but not always* accurate. That means you can't rely on the book value given in your statements for tax purposes in non-registered accounts: you must track it yourself. An example of where book value is usually wrong is if a stock or fund is merged with another, or changes its name: sometimes the book value updates to the value on the day the change happened rather than what you actually paid for your original holding. It will also be wrong if you have any transactions that adjust your cost basis, such as a superficial loss or a "return of capital" distribution.

Note that if you have a summary of fees paid, these are just the administrative fees such as charges for small accounts or direct trading costs like commissions. The MERs of your funds will not appear on your monthly statement, you will only find these by looking for them in the descriptions of the funds themselves.

Yearly trade summaries for non-registered accounts come out in the early spring to help you prepare for tax season. They are best used as a checklist to make sure you didn't miss any transactions in your record-keeping through the year rather than as your sole source for updating your records and reporting capital gains.

Tax documents will provide your dividends, interest, and other payments through the year in convenient boxes for you to enter into your tax program. They also usually come with a summary of the payments from each fund that led to that taxable income. What you want to look for here is box 42: Return of Capital. In the attached summary you can see how much return of capital was generated by each fund, and enter that amount into your capital gains spreadsheet as an amount reducing your cost basis (what you paid). For the most part every other aspect of your tax documents is much more simple: just enter the values in each of the boxes into the corresponding part of your tax software.

If you have a non-registered account and signed up for electronic statements, be sure to check for your tax statements before filing your taxes. If you typically file your taxes early, keep in mind some slips may not arrive until April.

Example Statements from Each Firm

Tangerine: When a statement is ready you'll get a notification in your "inbox" within the Tangerine web interface. They're also available from the "documents" section, found by clicking your name in the top-right corner. Note that your investing statements will show up about 10 days after your chequing and savings account statements – and for your first statement the placeholder for investment funds won't appear until about two weeks after the end of your first month with Tangerine.

As with everything at Tangerine, the statements are very minimalist and simple. There should only be a single portfolio fund in each of your accounts, and you will see a line item for each purchase or sale near the bottom of the summary listing the total amount, the unit price, and the number of units. They track the average cost per unit for you (book value), but as with all providers the ultimate responsibility is on your shoulders to accurately track it for tax purposes in a non-registered account. The opening and closing balance represent the market value at the beginning and end of the month.

John Robertson

tangerine.ca/investments

Mutual Funds at a Glance

Account Type	Account Number	Opening Balance($)	Closing Balance($)
Non-Registered Mutual Fund Account		0.00	102.01

The Details - Non-Registered Mutual Fund Account -

Account Registration:

Tangerine Equity Growth Portfolio
Average Cost per Unit: $ 14.0700   Percentage of Holdings: 100.00 %

Trade Date	Amount($)	Unit Price($)	No. of Units	Value($)
Opening Balance			0.0000	0.00
April 17, 2014 you purchased	101.00	14.0700	7.1784	101.00
April 30, 2014 Closing Balance		14.2100	7.1784	102.01

TD: You can access your electronic statements – including monthly statements, trade confirmations, and tax documents – by clicking on the "Accounts" tab in the top menu bar, then "Documents (eServices)" option (last one on the left). . TD will provide separate but very similar-looking statements for each of your accounts. On the first page will be a high-level overview of your holdings, with a box on the left side indicating how your portfolio is split up (which you can largely ignore as you will track your asset allocation more precisely yourself), and on the right side a box including lots of useful information like how much you have earned in dividends over the month and year-to-date, how much you have paid in fees and commissions, and for registered accounts, a summary of your contributions and withdrawals. Then any transactions will be listed, followed by a summary of your current portfolio (which will likely run onto the second page).

Some transactions to watch out for, especially in non-registered accounts, are reinvested dividends (DRIP). These don't generate trade confirmations, so the monthly statement is the only place they will show up. Below, I've included a sample of one of my statements with some TD e-series funds with reinvested dividends. Notice that

172

under the far-right column there is nothing for "credit" – these units are being purchased directly from the distribution as it happens. Under price "DRIP" appears to designate that it is a reinvested dividend, and the price itself appears in the second line under description. So for the first one, I had 4.635 units of the TD e-series Canadian Index purchased for me at a total value of $97.33. Where did that $97.33 come from? It was the December distribution (dividend) from my TD e-series Canadian index holdings.

			TRANSACTIONS DURING PERIOD				
Settlement Date	Bought or Received	Sold or Delivered	Description	Price and/or Entry	Amount		
						Debit	Credit
10/12/16	4.635		TD CDN INDX -E /NL'FRAC VALUE = 97.33	DRIP			0.00
10/12/16	1.033		TD US INDX C$ -E /NL'FRAC VALUE = 22.51	DRIP			0.00
10/12/16	2.844		TD INTL IDX E SER/NL'FRAC VALUE = 25.62	DRIP			0.00

Questrade: Their statements are broken up into multiple sections across several pages. This gives you multiple views into what your account is doing and can help with understanding what is happening – though it does use a lot of paper if you choose to print them off. They provide a breakdown of your allocation between cash and ETFs, but don't break down the ETFs into their own asset classes (Canadian versus international equities, etc.), though the second page of the *Investment Details* section will detail your allocation item-by-item (excluding cash).

Their *Activity Details* section is where you will find most of the important information you need. First is a *cash changes* page that groups your various transaction types together, including purchases, deposits, commissions and fees, dividends, etc. to give you a quick at-a-glace picture of the activity in your account.

Following that is the transactions list, which will be useful for tracking your purchases and sales for tax purposes. Canadian and US dollar transactions are clearly separated into different columns. The quantity ("Qty") and price per unit ("Price") are pretty self-explanatory, as is the commission ("Com") column. The "Gross" column represents the total amount invested before commissions and fees – simply quantity times price per unit – and purchases appear as negative amounts (in brackets). The net amount then is the book value for the purchase, including commssions.

QUESTRADE®

Transactions

Activity details

Trans. date¹	Settle date¹	Activity type	Symbol	Description	CAD					USD			
					Qty	Price	Gross¹	Com.¹	Net¹	Price	Gross¹	Com.¹	Net¹
4/17/2014	4/23/2014	Buy	VDU	VANGUARD FTSE DEVELOPED EX NORTH AMERICA INDX ETFR UNIT WE ACTED AS AGENT AVG PRICE. ASK US FOR DETAILS	121	28.610	(3,461.81)	(0.42)	(3,462.23)				

QUESTRADE®

Exchange traded funds Owned

	CURRENT MONTH			PREVIOUS MONTH		
	Securities held in CAD	Securities held in USD	Combined in CAD¹	Securities held in CAD	Securities held in USD	Combined in CAD¹
Market value ($)	3,492.06	-	3,492.06	-	-	-

Symbol	Description	Cost basis¹	Qty	Segr.¹	Cost/share	Pos. cost¹	Mkt. price¹	Mkt. value¹	P&L¹	% return¹	% port.¹
	Securities held in CAD										
VDU	VANGUARD FTSE DEVELOPED EX NORTH AMERICA INDX ETFR UNIT	BK	121	121	28.61	3,462.23	28.86	3,492.06	29.83	0.86	87.3

In addition to the general information on portfolio allocation and returns, you may wish to refer to the *Position Details* section, particularly the *Exchange Traded Funds Owned* page, which will detail the book value and market value of your ETF holdings. This table holds much of the same information covered in the other companies' statements. One unique addition is a column called "Cost basis" that indicates what method Questrade is using to report the cost or book value in your statements – their "BK" (book) method indicates that it will account for return-of-capital distributions. I will again note that the ultimate responsibility lies with you to ensure everything is tracked and reported to the Canada Revenue Agency correctly.

To translate the other column headings, "cost/share" is the per-share book value or cost basis, including any commissions or ECN fees. "Position cost" is the total book value, "Mkt. price" and "Mkt. value" are the per-share and total market values as of when the statement was prepared (usually the last trading day of the month). The "P&L" column takes the difference between market and book values for you, to show you in dollars and cents how much you are up (or down) on your investments – note that this is your unrealized or "paper" gain/loss, and you would need to pay a selling commission before being able to collect that money, in addition to any day-to-day or minute-to-minute changes in value on the exchanges. The next column "% return" simply puts this profit/loss into a percentage of the book value, and "% port" is how much this holding represents of the overall portfolio.

Expected Value and Process

We always have to make decisions in life with imperfect information; we cannot predict the future with any great deal of accuracy. In hindsight, you may be able to say that investing in banks and gold miners was the optimal strategy, and everything else in the index was just weighing you down, or that US and international investments should have been a stronger weighting. But in advance, it is nearly impossible to make these kinds of calls correctly and consistently. So diversifying broadly helps protect us against surprises and bad guesses, and best work towards an acceptable expected value.

Similarly, some people will luck into mutual funds that earn more than their fee in returns and out-perform a passive indexing approach. Most, however, won't. So the best decision to make *in advance* is to avoid the mutual fund fees, control your costs and your complexity, and invest in index funds.

You cannot control outcomes, except to position yourself to make the best decisions you can with the information available at the time, to maximize your *expected* value and protect yourself from some of the most likely sources of failure. Processes are very important for long-term success. I have the following quotation from John Hempton enshrined on my desktop: "...I realized that the processes were as important as the outcome. *Indeed they are more important.*"[77]

---

[77] John Hempton from the Bronte Capital blog, January 20, 2009:
http://brontecapital.blogspot.ca/2009/01/slogan-for-new-administration.html

A good process will help you best position yourself for the uncertain future, and adapt as outcomes change. Sometimes you will be wrong based on the outcome. For instance, if you split your investments half into bonds and half into stocks, and then see stocks crash. But based on what you knew at the time, that was a good choice to make, and you would make it again after the crash – so you rebalance, and buy more stock.

Trying to over-complicate, over-fit, over-optimize, or over-manage your investments is not a good approach to create a sustainable process. A common error is to have such a revulsion to paying tax that people jump into convoluted schemes and products that end up losing them money on the whole. For example, don't buy money-losing rental properties in order to get a tax deduction. Losing money is losing money, and hating tax so much that you'd rather lose $5 yourself to avoid having to give $1 of it to the government is irrational.

Accepting that information and estimates are imperfect and adapting as the situation changes is a key component of a good process. If you were driving along a road and saw a stop sign, you might estimate that you need 100 feet to stop smoothly. When you see that you're close to 100 feet away you would apply the brake and continue to watch and adjust – you would not just apply the initial estimate of pressure, close your eyes, and hope to wake up 10 seconds later behind the line rather than in the intersection.

So too with investing: if after ten years you see your savings rate is not keeping you on track to meet your long-term goals, you can adjust it. I have laid out some rules of thumb and information to help you create good investing processes to work towards your future dreams.

Your processes should be:

- Easy to implement, not rely on overly accurate forecasting of the future.

- Have minimal moving parts, record keeping, and other requirements.

- Adaptable, with pre-determined responses to crises.

- Allow for multiple outcomes, rather than betting exclusively on one.

- Focused. Control what can be controlled.

Turning Investments into Retirement Income

For most people, the ultimate goal of all this planning and investing activity is to set themselves up for a future where they are not working. At some point, the task will be turning investments into retirement income. This is more complicated than saving and investing, requires more precision, and is worthy of a book in its own right.

To be clear, the basic mechanics are not any more difficult: instead of saving and adding money every month or year to your portfolio and doing the rebalancing, you will sell some and live off the proceeds. However, there are a number of factors that you have to consider more carefully in retirement, in part because of the situation, and in part because the particulars do not fade away in the mists of future uncertainty – there is less ability to start off approximately right and correct later.

Young people may not necessarily need outside help from a financial planner or advisor – with what was covered earlier in the book you can invest on your own, and a more detailed plan may not be worth the money when there is so much unavoidable future uncertainty ahead of you[78]. For near-retirees however, a visit to a financial planner or advisor can be well worth the fee. Turning your investments into retirement income carries many special considerations, including:

- Sequence-of-returns risk.

- Longevity risk.

---

[78] But when you need help planning, or help budgeting, then an advisor may be worth the cost at any age.

- Tax and benefit considerations, such as when to convert your RRSP to an RRIF, or when to take or defer OAS and CPP.

- Balancing a legacy with optimal spending and whether to buy an annuity.

- Choosing to sell or downsize your house.

- Different spending patterns, and differences between your personal inflation rate and the official inflation averages.

- The strategy and approach for viewing your investment portfolio.

- Whether it is preferable to be conservative with spending and get a steady retirement income, or to spend more but allow market returns to dictate your spending capacity.

Surveys show that most people spend less as retirement goes on – however, the surveys don't tell us whether this is a feature of their plan or a failure[79]. Using a constant, average figure for your income needs makes planning more straightforward, but may not be realistic: even if you don't plan for a gradual tapering in spending as you travel less, there will likely be irregular expenses like repairs, health care, or new cars.

Your personal inflation rate may differ from the official one used by the government and your pension plan to adjust your benefits, known as the consumer price index (CPI). In your working and saving years, you likely have a spending pattern similar to the average person's that

---

[79] Michael Wiener did find one study that suggests indeed, spending reductions are forced on retirees by their circumstances. He discusses it at

http://www.michaeljamesonmoney.com/2014/02/telling-us-what-we-want-to-hear-about.html

makes up the CPI inflation calculation, and your income will likely rise along with inflation. In retirement your spending may be concentrated in certain categories, for instance you may spend most of your money on food and energy, and not spend anything on furniture, having already acquired a lifetime supply. So if what you spend your money on (food & energy) increase in price while what you don't (furniture) decreases, your *personal* inflation rate may considerably outstrip the official CPI calculation, and so this can be a much larger risk factor in retirement.

Focusing on your investments and getting income out of them, there are several ways to approach your portfolio as you enter retirement.

The simplest is to simply continue as you did in your accumulation years, with a steady shift towards fixed income to reduce the potential volatility; sell what you need and what your plan dictates to get cash each year, and rebalance periodically. There is a common "rule" for how much to withdraw from such an approach, which is to take 4% (less about half the fees) of your starting portfolio to spend, and increase the amount with inflation each year. For example, if you were paying 0.4% in MERs by investing in e-series index funds and had $500,000 on the day you retired, you would withdraw 3.8% of that, or $19,000, to spend in the first year – increasing the amount each year with inflation. Such a simple rule has a lot of appeal, which may explain its popularity, but there are downsides. It's good enough for most historical market conditions, but still particularly sensitive to a big crash right after setting your withdrawal rate – it may be better to use a more responsive strategy right from the beginning. Conversely, to meet the "most market conditions" criteria, it's overly conservative for many scenarios (though that is not such a bad problem to have).

Another popular option is to shift to a portfolio of dividend-paying stocks and "live off the dividends". I am not fond of this strategy. On the one hand, if you are only living off the dividends then you are being needlessly conservative in your spending, as dividends are just one component of total return. Unless you have a strong desire to leave a large legacy, you should plan to spend a bit of your capital. It is also a strategy that involves too much equity risk, and concentrating to just a few sectors that tend to pay dividends, rather than diversifying broadly. It swings to becoming too risky if there's a concentration in a small selection of companies paying high (and unsustainable) dividends.

Another method that is worth considering is a "bucket" approach. In this method you split your future years' spending needs into "buckets" that you can fill with different sub-portfolios. For example, you could have a bucket for the current year and following year's spending budget, held in savings accounts and ready to spend as needed. The next few years, say years 2-10, could be held in bond funds and GICs with appropriate maturities. The rest, for ten years out and into the more distant future, could be invested largely in equity funds, or a portfolio appropriate to the time available and your risk tolerance. In future years, depending on the performance of your investments, you can adjust filling the next mid-term spending bucket from your long-term bucket. This lets your budget respond to changes in investment performance, but with a bit of a lag so you have time to ease your spending and lifestyle into it.

At this point you may easily be thinking that things would be so much easier with a defined benefit pension plan: you would have a set level of income – likely adjusted for inflation each year – that would last until you died, taking care of longevity risk. An annuity (specifically a *life annuity*) is a way to approximate[80] the benefits of a pension yourself. By paying a lump sum near retirement, an insurance company can guarantee a steady stream of payments for the rest of your life, no matter how long you may live. The cost of that assurance is that if you die young, there may be nothing left of that lump sum for your family, friends, or favourite charity to inherit.

---

[80] Inflation protection is less common in annuities.

Worked Examples

Here are two worked examples to help you apply the lessons.

Long-term Adjustments: Petra

When Petra graduates from university she has some debt to pay off, and takes a few years to find her feet in her career in the midst of her world travels. On her thirtieth birthday her dad announces his imminent retirement, and she has an epiphany as she realizes she hasn't thought about her own. Unlike her father's generation, she will not be able to count on a company pension to take care of her – it will be up to her and her savings to make it work.

She comes up with a simple plan, makes a few modest cuts to her spending so she can start to save, and builds an emergency fund in the first year of saving. The next year she starts investing, following the default allocation of having her age less 10 in bonds – now at age 31, she starts with 21% in bonds – and the rest split equally into a Canadian, US, and international fund. She starts by investing $5,000 each year, and increases that 2% each year with inflation.

Though she starts with tempered expectations of how investing will provide returns on a yearly basis, the first few years knock her socks off. Unlike a dull savings account at her bank, her stock portfolio has *rocketed* higher! At year 5 her modest savings have already turned into nearly $43,000, which only took $26,020 from her pocket!

The good times were not to last, however. Three bad years hit shortly after she started investing: her three equity index funds lost on average 3%, 12%, and 17% those years, but with the bonds to cushion it her overall portfolio was flat the first year, and only down 6% and 11% in the next two years. Her rate of return was less in the recovery that followed because once again bonds lagged stock returns, but because she had less to recover, it would take an all-stock portfolio 11 years to catch up to her more appropriately balanced investments.

Though the stocks out-performed initially and bonds looked like a major drag, deciding to change her plan and reduce her bond holdings because they were underperforming equities after a good 5-year run would have been a mistake for Petra. The bonds played an important role in reducing volatility, which made it much easier for her to stick to her plan through all the ups and downs (well, mostly the downs).

The next decade featured two market crashes, filling the media with stories of fear and a rigged system. The reality, while not quite meeting Petra's original plan, was not so grim: her portfolio crossed $200,000 as she turned 50. Despite the doom and gloom in the news about a lost decade, she's only about $12,000 behind where she had planned to be at this age – a relatively small amount that doesn't necessarily signal a problem in her plan worth addressing. Nonetheless, Petra thinks that saving too much is a better problem to have than coming up short, so she increases her monthly savings by $100/mo. It's actually an easy adjustment for her, because she had only been increasing her monthly contributions with the inflation rate, while her actual salary had been rising faster than that as she moved up the corporate ladder at work.

Despite the ups and downs of the market over the years, Petra finds that sticking to her plan and tuning out the noise has put her in a fairly decent position for the future, and has the opportunity in the home stretch to make a relatively easy adjustment to stay on course.

Advanced Details on Return-of-Capital: Alex

Alex is pretty financially responsible for a 26-year-old, having made it through school with next to no debt. He's taken his family's advice about living within his means and paying himself first to heart, and as soon as his debts were paid off he set up a non-registered and TFSA savings account and an automatic monthly contribution. He never carries a balance on his credit cards, and he has a dedicated account where he's saving up for his next car so he can minimize any borrowing for that. As soon as January 2nd, 2014 rolls around he sets up a transfer from his non-registered account to his TFSA version to max out his new $5,500 in TFSA room right at the beginning of the year. From the time TFSAs were introduced to now, he's contributed $31,000, and thanks to the interest he's earned, his account is worth $32,155 after the contribution takes effect in early January.

But he isn't invested in anything more productive than high-interest savings accounts. He got a copy of this book to read over summer vacation in June, 2014. He takes a weekend to review his plan, and realizes that his investments don't match his risk tolerance at all. He opens a Questrade account and prepares to invest in ETFs. He decides that he wants to get started right away, and will use the TFSA shuffle to avoid paying a $150 transfer-out fee from his bank. With the interest earned over the first half of 2014, he has $32,390 to withdraw in June.

At 26, he decides that rounding off to a 20% bond allocation would work for him, and that he will evenly split his equity portion between Canada, the US, and international markets. He doesn't have much RRSP room accumulated yet, and believes that in the next ten years he will be making more at his job and move up into the next tax bracket. So he focuses just on his TFSA for now.

Renting a condo in Vancouver, Alex decides that he will modify the basic asset allocation scheme a bit to include some real estate investment trusts (REITs), tinkering a little bit with core-and-explore. Though he thinks that one day he will decide to own the roof over his head, buying is not something he plans to do in the near-term. After all, he sees all the stories in the news about a potential housing bubble, and even the ones that dismiss the idea start with "except for Vancouver, Canada doesn't have a housing bubble..." Plus he's done the rent-versus-buy math himself to find that renting is the smart choice at those nose-bleed prices. That means all of these savings can be targeted to the long term. He decides to go with the iShares XRE ETF for his REIT exposure, and that it will count as part of his Canadian equity allocation.

With $32,390 in cash now in his non-registered account, his asset allocation plan looks like this:

Asset Class	Product	% Weight	$ to Invest (rounded)	Unit Price	# Units to Buy
Bonds	XQB	20%	$6,478	$20.24	319
Canadian Equity	XIC XRE	20% 6.66%	$6,478 $2,157	$22.99 $16.19	281 133
US Equity	VUN	26.67%	$8,638	$28.97	297
International Equity	XEF	26.67%	$8,638	$28.72	300

As he converts from the amount he would like to buy to the number of units, he holds back $10 just in case to cover ECN fees or commissions, in addition to the buffer that comes from rounding down. He enters his limit orders and finds they all fill within minutes.

In January of 2015 he gets his TFSA contribution room back – the $32,390 withdrawn in the previous year – along with an additional $5,500. He calls his account representative at Questrade to make an "in-kind" contribution and puts all of his holdings into the TFSA. Of course, the value has fluctuated over the few months, and the value the contribution is made at depends on the new market value. Alex will have to report any capital gains based on increases in value relative to the contribution because these are "deemed distributions." Here is how that looks.

Prices as of January 2015 (those used for the in-kind contribution):

XQB, $20.20/unit.

XIC, $23.80/unit.

XRE, $17.33/unit.

VUN, $28.10/unit.

XEF, $26.75/unit.

If XQB, VUN, and XEF are lower than when he purchased them then there will be no capital gains to pay. Because of the superficial loss rule he will not be able to claim the capital loss from an in-kind contribution to his TFSA.

In addition to the change in value, he finds that on his T3 tax slip, XRE paid a return-of-capital distribution (box 42). He subtracts this from his cost base before reporting the gain. Here is his own spreadsheet that he uses for tracking:

Date	Fund Name/Symbol	Units Purchased	Total Purchase	Fees	Cost Basis
June 30, 2014	REIT Index, XRE	133	$2,153.27	$0.50	$2,153.77
Dec 31, 2014	XRE		* return of capital for 2014		($0.67)
Dec 31, 2014	XRE		* calculated net cost basis for in-kind contribution to TFSA in January		$2,153.10
Jan 2, 2015	XRE		* transfer out to TFSA		$2,304.89

The capital gains then go into his tax software under Schedule 3 for the 2015 tax year:

Schedule 3

# Shares	Name of Fund	Year of Acq	Proceeds of Disposition	Adjusted Cost Base	Outlays and Expenses	Gain (or loss)
133	XRE	2014	2,304.89	2,153.10		151.79
281	XIC	2014	6,687.80	6,460.69		227.11

Note that the return of capital was miniscule in this case, but to be proper had to be tracked. Nothing was entered under outlays and expenses as he had included the ECN fees and commissions (if applicable) for purchasing in the adjusted cost base, and there was no fee for the in-kind transfer – if instead Alex had sold the funds and paid a commission, that could have been entered into outlays and expenses, or simply incorporated into the proceeds of disposition.

Half of the $378.90 capital gain will be added to his income (the calculation of which will be handled by the tax software).

Now that everything has been moved into his TFSA, Alex no longer needs to track his cost basis or report any capital gains on his taxes. While the whole exercise was very educational in understanding how to track and report his investment gains, in hindsight Alex wonders if he should have just paid the transfer-out fee.

Next Steps

Investing can be simple. It is a natural fit for a straightforward, easy, hands-off approach. Intervening in your portfolio as little as possible and keeping your costs low are the keys to success, and also aspects that will help you spend as little time and energy on it as possible – after all, most people only want to get their money working for them to achieve some other goal like a comfortable retirement, and beyond that it should be as unobtrusive as possible. At this point I hope you have the knowledge, tools, and confidence to set out and start investing on your own.

Take a moment for reflection to be sure that you're in a position to invest. Here are some things to consider:

- Do you have high-interest debt you should be paying off first?

- Are you living within your means, with savings to invest?

- Have you disaster-proofed your life, which may include saving an emergency fund and securing whatever insurance coverage you may need?

If you're ready to invest, then move on while the information is still fresh in your mind and the motivation is strong. Sort out the why, what, where, how, who, and when of your investment plan.

Why are you investing? Though this can be very nebulous as you start, having a goal in mind will help determine your risk tolerance, and will be something to focus on if times get tough. Better yet, a complete plan will form the framework into which your investing will fit.

What will you invest in? Your asset allocation will determine the main balance between risk and potential returns. I've provided some simple rules-of-thumb to get a diversified portfolio set up in minutes, covering four major asset classes.

Where will you place your funds? Many people will be able to keep all of their investments inside a tax-sheltered account such as a TFSA, RRSP, or RESP. That will simplify tracking and reporting. If you can't fill all of them, which will be the priority for you based on your situation? Will you worry about optimizing, trying to put some classes into certain places (like US equities into your RRSP), or just reproduce the same basic portfolio in each account? Also consider which firm you will use, and the trade-offs between ETFs and mutual funds in terms of cost and complexity.

How will you manage as the years go on? Consider your rebalancing strategy, savings plan, and tracking spreadsheets or other programs. How will you adjust your plan in the future when markets inevitably provide returns that differ from your initial estimates, or your life circumstances change?

Who will you turn to for support, and when? If you don't need an advisor to choose and manage funds for you, do you still need to hire an expert to help you with a plan or your cash flow? A support network of friends, family, or even internet buddies can be invaluable to bounce ideas off of, and to help keep you on track.

When can you start? When will you take a pause to review your plan in detail and adjust if necessary?

Once you have your plan in place and some savings gathered – as little as a few hundred dollars to start with index mutual funds, but over $5,000 is a better starting place for ETFs to avoid account inactivity fees – then it's time to open an account and get started!

Control what can be controlled. Minimize your costs, effort, and room for human error. Remember the value of simple: investing doesn't have to be complex or time-consuming, and paying a bit more in fees or for professional advice may be worth it in the end. Trust your processes and plans – especially through the hard times.

You can do this.

Getting Help

Taking that first step to making your first trade and maybe even leaving an existing salesperson who isn't providing value for the commissions they take can be a scary thing. I hope that I have provided you with all the information and guidance you need to take that step of investing on your own. If you need more help, there are lots of resources out there.

Though some people who make their money through hidden commissions and trailer fees on mutual funds can provide worthwhile advice on cash flow planning, estate advice, and help you create a detailed financial plan, it is a business model that lets far too many people down. In my opinion the large banks and firms are too focused on sales targets and products that they sell[81] and their training isn't robust enough to help their clients in the best way possible. And unfortunately, it is very difficult to know who to trust if you don't yourself have so much knowledge that you could just do it yourself in the first place.

The industry's business model has done a disservice to people: the focus on selling investments and insurance has led people to believe that those are all financial advice *is* – and that if you don't have an insurance need or money to invest, then you don't need (or can't use) an advisor/planner. Plus the typical method of making the advice part look free by burying the costs in products fees or commissions devalues planning and advice, when really a plan – and the conversations to develop that plan

---

[81] For a longer version of this rant, see
http://www.holypotato.net/?p=1750

– can be hugely valuable, while the service of picking and managing the investments can be straightforward and not worth the fees typically paid for it.

If you can now handle the investing portion of your finances, but need help with cash flow management and planning, a money coach can be an excellent option. If you need more financial planning, a fee-only or fee-for-service financial planner can help.

I wish there was a single designation or firm I could point you towards with a strong recommendation, secure in the knowledge that they would have the ethics and expertise to help. In my opinion, the embedded commission model creates too many conflicts-of-interest; psychologically the fact that it is hidden even helps lower the likelihood that you will consider what your advisor does objectively and whether they provide value. In recent years the UK and Australia have banned such commissions, and some of us here in Canada are pushing for similar reforms. Those who have willingly thrown aside that model are the ones I think will most likely provide the value and ethics in planning. I've created a directory of such planners at http://directory.valueofsimple.ca

Unfortunately, there still aren't very many planners who charge directly for their services, so it will be a lot easier to find someone if you're willing to work remotely (which many planners are).

When you're looking for someone to help, be sure to ask lots of questions – including how they get paid, how their interests align with yours, and what you should get out of it – before signing on with a planner. The focus is very often put on investing because of how foreign it is to most people – and because selling investments may be how the advisor gets paid (or because the view is not to serve the needs of the person and their holistic life where money is important, but to serve the needs of the money – that "the client is the money"[82]). However, this is where advisors provide the least amount of value. You should now be able to handle your investments all on your own, so you can focus on cash flow, budgeting, behaviour, trade-offs and lifestyle, values and goals, planning, wills, insurance, or tax optimization with your advisor.

There are also questions of how you want to work with a planner. Are you looking to have a one-off engagement to discuss some particular issue or get a plan created, or are you looking for an ongoing support or subscription model?

Though I haven't worked with them personally in their professional capacity, Sandi Martin is a fee-for-service advisor who has experience working as a salesperson at a bank, and now runs her own business (www.springplans.ca/). I like a lot of what I see Money Coaches Canada doing in terms of their processes (moneycoachescanada.ca/), and have had a number of intelligent conversations with Noel D'Souza of Toronto. Chris Enns started Rags to Reasonable (ragstoreasonable.com) to help people with variable income, particularly artists. Dan Bortolotti, is another advocate of passive index investing in Canada (he even wrote his own book on the matter, called *The MoneySense Guide to the Perfect Portfolio*). He has teamed up with PWL Capital to offer a fee-based service. And there are many more great fee-for-service and fee-based advisors, coaches, and planners out there.

---

[82] An observation from Sandi Martin, written about by Chris Enns here: https://www.ragstoreasonable.com/talking-money/

Further Reading

I've tried to keep this book short and to the point. The passive index investing strategy that aims to minimize fees is well-supported and is a good option for nearly any investor. There's really no need to present options that I'm not going to recommend in the end anyway, or to beat you over the head with data attempting to prove why you should invest this way. That would make the book too long – as it is, I hope that you can finish it in just a few sittings and then actually get off your butt and start saving and investing.

But now you're at the end and perhaps you'd like to read more, or want to see the evidence to back up what I've been saying, or just get a second opinion. And there's plenty of material to read on investing! I've created a reading guide infographic you can download at http://www.holypotato.net/?p=1327, with a few selected titles below:

Budgeting/Saving

Worry-Free Money by Shannon Lee Simmons describes how you can set up your finances to make sure your major goals are met and your money is working to help make you happy. Once the big things are taken care of, the method she describes lets you spend the rest worry-free.

Gail Vaz-Oxlade (www.gailvazoxlade.com) is one of the big names in telling people how to get their spending under control, and her website has a collection of articles, quizzes, and rules-of-thumb, so that's another good place to start.

The Wealthy Barber Returns by David Chilton is a great general introduction to money topics, like saving for the future, staying out of debt, and understanding how your RRSP and TFSA can help you. It's very conversational and full of examples.

Stop Over-Thinking Your Money by Preet Banerjee covers five simple rules for getting your finances on track. In particular, his section on disaster-proofing your life is worth reading for its detailed guide to buying life and disability insurance, and the importance thereof.

Wealthing Like Rabbits by Rob Brown provides a light-hearted, pop-culture-reference-packed take on personal finance. The alternate timeline view of how decisions like buying more house than you can afford are really clear tales on the importance of these decisions, not just in dollars, but in the stress that money can have on your life.

Millionaire Teacher by Andrew Hallam crosses over between budgeting/saving and investing for the long term. In addition to more talk about why an indexing approach is best, he discusses how millionaires are more likely to be frugal, and what wealth and financial independence are.

Your local library should also have some good books on setting a budget, with tricks to stick to it (ask your librarian for what's available near you). Libraries and the continuing studies arms of various universities also often have lectures on personal finance and financial literacy.

If you'd like personalized help, many finance blogs, newspapers, and forums are looking for case studies to examine, and can help you create a budget in the process. Or for more in-depth personalized help, a money coach can help you better manage your finances.

Passive/Index Investing

Dan Bortolotti, aka the Canadian Couch Potato (no relation) has a blog at canadiancouchpotato.com where he discusses passive investing, and updates his readers on the performance of various passive portfolios vs the regular mutual fund industry and the industry research on investing in general (but especially that evidence that backs up the concept of index investing with low fees). He also has several tools to help the passive investor, including several "model portfolios" built from mutual funds and ETFs (which are not meaningfully different from the selection of funds offered earlier in the book). He has also written a book titled *The MoneySense Guide to the Perfect Portfolio*.

The Little Book of Common Sense Investing by John C. Bogle is a reasonably short book, but is written for Americans (so you'll need at the least my information on our tax shelters and how to get to TD's e-series funds or Canadian ETFs). It contains a fair bit more information on *why* you should choose index investing over other styles, and is an easy read.

A Random Walk Down Wall Street by Burton Malkiel is a much longer book, but contains a lot more historical information, and also makes a strong case for *why* you should choose a passive investing strategy. Though most of the information is pretty general, it is again from an American perspective so specific information about their mutual fund industry doesn't quite apply to Canadians.

Behavioural Finance

Your own behaviour and feelings towards *stuff*, spending money, and investing are incredibly important factors in charting your way to long-term success. Understanding some of the shortcuts your brain takes in processing, and the biases that result, can help prepare you to overcome them.

Dan Ariely's *Predictably Irrational* is excellent. In particular, the sections covering the problem with free and how you unconsciously treat relationships that involve a monetary exchange are very relevant to how people see their financial advisors, and why MERs on mutual funds being hidden is so critical to that business model's success. Of course, once you realize that your advisor is getting paid out of your pocket – just in a hidden way – then there can often be feelings of betrayal leading to an instant, irreversible breakdown (and a welcome to self-directed investing).

Freakonomics is a popular and easy read touching on the subject, with several follow-ups from Steven Levitt and Stephen Dubner.

The *Undoing Project* by Michael Lewis is more biography than how-to, but it's very readable and does touch on many important aspects.

Misbehaving by Richard Thaler covers many important aspects of behaviour finances, from the winner of the Nobel Prize for economics.

Happy Money by Elizabeth Dunn and Michael Norton look at what sort of spending will help lead to greater happiness

Active Investing

There are some that believe that the returns from investing in the market indexes cannot be improved upon, that is, that you *can't* beat the index except by luck. That not only is passive investing a good strategy which is also easy and practical, but that it is the only strategy that should be considered. To be sure, some people/funds will beat the index, but, the argument goes, you can't tell who those people will be *in advance*. Others argue that the index can be beaten, and there are tonnes of books about investing that try to tell you how to search for stocks that can do it. Even if you stick with a passive investing approach, they have some good lessons on business and investing, and above all, thinking logically and independently.

It is my opinion that it is not *impossible* to beat the index, but that it is *difficult enough* that the average investor will do better by not attempting it – simply follow a passive investing strategy as described above. If you would like to learn more about the dark side though, here are some books to start with:

The Little Book of Value Investing by Chris Browne is another from the "little book of..." series, and describes why a value investing strategy has a chance of beating the index, and how to go about value investing. This book, as well as others, can also be a good read even for a passive investor, as it can help teach the lesson that a downturn is a time to buy, not to sell (rebalancing will help you do this mechanically), and to understand the process that the active investors go through (and why you want to have nothing to do with it).

A search for an old article by Warren Buffet called "*the Superinvestors of Graham-and-Doddsville*" will describe why he believes value investing can and does beat the passive index methods (though note that Warren himself recommends that the average investor should just buy the index as most people make poor active investors!)

The Intelligent Investor by Ben Graham (recent versions revised by Jason Zweig or Janet Lowe) is a must-read for anyone attempting fundamental analysis and value investing.

Other Resources

Canadian Money Forum (canadianmoneyforum.com) is a forum that discusses a variety of investment and other money topics like budgeting and frugality. It's a good resource to turn to if you have any questions along the way. Similarly, Reddit has a Personal Finance Canada group (www.reddit.com/r/PersonalFinanceCanada/) that is full of people ready to help review short case studies and answer any specific questions you may have about investing.

Sandi Martin and I worked together to create a program that we get invited to a branch of the Toronto Public Library about once a year to present[83]. Other cities will have their own set of resources through their universities, colleges, and libraries.

Blessed by the Potato (www.holypotato.net) is my own personal blog. I often write about investing and financial topics, and have developed several spreadsheet-based tools for the community (some of which are linked at appropriate places in the book). The blog is a great way to keep in touch with me, though you can email me too – invest@therobertsons.net.

To keep up-to-date on changes relevant to the book, appearances, and more, be sure to sign up for my mailing list – you can find a form on the book's website, or directly at http://eepurl.com/7gmP9 – it's a relatively quiet email list, expect 4-6 messages per year.

If you've made it this far and are still looking for more details on how to be a do-it-yourself investor, then you should look at my online course, *Practical Index Investing,* which you can find at http://course.valueofsimple.ca. The course has over twice as much information as the book can hold, with a mix of text articles, presentations, and videos to help teach the material, plus the questions and answers that a community of fellow students helps create.

Finally, remember to check the website for updates and corrections at ValueofSimple.ca.

---

[83] Though now I've probably jinxed it.

The End

Thank you for reading this. I hope you found it useful, and I wish you luck in your investing journey. Remember: save, invest, plan for the future, and act on your plan. Keep your costs low, your eyes open, and your investments diversified. It's better to get started early with a plan that's *close enough* than to wait years trying to come up with the *perfect* plan and lose out on all that time.

I wish you the best of luck, and may your money compound like bunnies.

Acknowledgements

I'd like to thank a lot of people for their help with the book. I worked closely with Drew Salter and Jill Bressmer to create and implement investment plans, and it was largely through the experience of working with and teaching them that I realized what needed to be in this book; indeed that a book like this was needed in the first place. From my old home at the Lawson Health Research Institute, Samantha Brown provided proof-reading of the initial short guide, Dr. Julia McKay provided feedback and the inspiration of her pet bunny Kiwi, while Dr. John Patrick provided the photographs of said bunny. Katherine Robertson also reviewed the first draft of that book. As that little project matured into a full book, I have to thank my editorial team and beta readers:

- Jill Bressmer, creationbodypiercing.ca

- Dr. Carrie-Lynn Keiski

- Dr. Margaret Kinyanjui

- Kelly Robertson

- Ben Pakuts, benpakuts.com, also responsible for the wonderful cover

- Sandi Martin, springplans.ca and becausemoney.ca

- Kyle Prevost, freelance personal finance writer for youngandthrifty.ca and other sites

- Shelly, savespendsplurge.com

- Michael Wiener, michaeljamesonmoney.com

- Chris Enns, ragstoreasonable.com (for reviewing 2nd edition changes)

I'd also like to thank Kyle Prevost, Preet Banerjee, Melissa Leong, and Erin Vollick for discussions on the publishing process.

And of course, my family: I have to thank my dad Bruce Robertson for teaching me about and getting me interested in investing at a young age, and Kelly Robertson for all of her help and patience. Especially Kelly for pushing me to keep the quality and effort up through the last mile, when I was ready to stamp it "good enough" and start shipping – and for stepping up to fill the Chief Marketing Officer role.

After publishing the first edition, I also have to give a **huge thank-you** to everyone who took time out of their day to leave a review, tell their friends, or recommend it in forums and articles. Books live and die on word-of-mouth and 5-star reviews, and the highly positive reviews and your heartfelt recommendations to your friends and family really helped make *The Value of Simple* a success. Thank you in advance for your support.

Data sources include: Yahoo Finance, Google Finance, and the incredible Norbert Schlenker and Libra Investment Management, who collected and compiled real-returns data on Canadian and international equities, adjusted to Canadian dollars. Also in turn their data sources: Statistics Canada; Prof. Werner Antweiler, UBC; the Bank of Canada; BC Government Statistics; the Financial Post; the Globe & Mail; Scotia Capital; the Canadian Institute of Actuaries; Economagic.com; Standard & Poors; and MSCI.

About the Author

John Robertson is a scientist, writer, investor, teacher, and massive fan of em-dashes. He has a PhD from the University of Western Ontario in Medical Biophysics, and spends his days as a science writer & editor for the Techna Institute in Toronto, part of the University Health Network. Winner of multiple scientific presentation awards and the Macklin Teaching Fellowship from the University of Western Ontario, he specializes in explaining complex topics – scientific or financial – for the lay reader.

He is a co-host of the Because Money podcast (becausemoney.ca) and teaches investing online (course.valueofsimple.ca). He has also been invited to give public talks at the Toronto Public Library and to be a guest speaker for two University of Toronto continuing education courses on investing.

John lives in Toronto with his wife, daughter, and the cat-shaped hole in their hearts. He also writes under the pen name of *Potato* at holypotato.net, a personal blog with a large focus on personal finance.

CPSIA information can be obtained
at www.ICGtesting.com
Printed in the USA
LVHW022214071019
633190LV00012BA/73/P

9 780987 818935